YORK I

CW01498272

Nights at the Circus

Angela Carter

Note by Ruth Robbins

 Longman   ⊙ York Press

Copyright © Angela Carter 1984. Reproduced by permission of the Estate of Angela Carter c/o Rogers, Coleridge & White Ltd., 20 Powis Mews, London W11 1JN

Ruth Robbins is hereby identified as author of this work in accordance with Section 77 of the Copyright, Designs and Patents Act 1988

YORK PRESS
322 Old Brompton Road, London SW5 9JH

PEARSON EDUCATION LIMITED
Edinburgh Gate, Harlow,
Essex CM20 2JE, United Kingdom
Associated companies, branches and representatives throughout the world

© Librairie du Liban *Publishers* and Pearson Education Limited 2000

All rights reserved. No part of this publication may be reproduced, stored in a retrieval system, or transmitted in any form or by any means, electronic, mechanical, photocopying, recording, or otherwise, without either the prior written permission of the Publishers or a licence permitting restricted copying in the United Kingdom issued by the Copyright Licensing Agency Ltd, 90 Tottenham Court Road, London W1P 9HE

First published 2000

ISBN 0-582-42451-8

Designed by Vicki Pacey
Phototypeset by Gem Graphics, Trenance, Mawgan Porth, Cornwall
Colour reproduction and film output by Spectrum Colour
Produced by Addison Wesley Longman China Limited, Hong Kong

CONTENTS

PART ONE

INTRODUCTION How to Study a Novel   5
              Reading *Nights at the Circus*   6

PART TWO

SUMMARIES & COMMENTARIES
              Note on the Text   8
              Synopsis   8
              Detailed Summaries   11
                Part One: London   11
                Part Two: Petersburg   29
                Part Three: Siberia   57

PART THREE

CRITICAL APPROACHES
              Characterisation   83
              Themes   85
                Reality and Illusion   85
                Humans and Animals   86
                Social and Economic Conditions   87
              Narrative Structure   87
                Time   87
                Repeating Structure   88
              Genre   89
              Language & Style   90
              Symbolism   92

PART FOUR

TEXTUAL ANALYSIS
              Text 1: Walser's Character   95
              Text 2: The Baboushka Tells a Story   98
              Text 3: Fevvers's Escape from   101
                the Grand Duke

PART FIVE

BACKGROUND

The Author and Her Works   **105**
Historical and Literary Background   **107**

PART SIX

CRITICAL HISTORY & BROADER PERSPECTIVES

Reception and Critical History   **111**
Contemporary Approaches
    Bakhtin and Foucault: **112**
      Cultural Theory in Action
    Marxist Approaches   **115**
    Feminist Approaches: **117**
      Écriture Féminine
Further Reading   **120**

Chronology   **123**
Literary Terms   **127**
Author of this Note   **132**

PART ONE

INTRODUCTION

HOW TO STUDY A NOVEL

Studying a novel on your own requires self-discipline and a carefully thought-out work plan in order to be effective.

- You will need to read the novel more than once. Start by reading it quickly for pleasure, then read it slowly and thoroughly.
- On your second reading make detailed notes on the plot, characters and themes of the novel. Further readings will generate new ideas and help you to memorise the details of the story.
- Some of the characters will develop as the plot unfolds. How do your responses towards them change during the course of the novel?
- Think about how the novel is narrated. From whose point of view are events described?
- A novel may or may not present events chronologically: the time-scheme may be a key to its structure and organisation.
- What part do the settings play in the novel?
- Are words, images or incidents repeated so as to give the work a pattern? Do such patterns help you to understand the novel's themes?
- Identify what styles of language are used in the novel.
- What is the effect of the novel's ending? Is the action completed and closed, or left incomplete and open?
- Does the novel present a moral and just world?
- Cite exact sources for all quotations, whether from the text itself or from critical commentaries. Wherever possible find your own examples from the novel to back up your opinions.
- Always express your ideas in your own words.

This York Note offers an introduction to *Nights at the Circus* and cannot substitute for close reading of the text and the study of secondary sources.

The classical definition of the purpose of literature, derived from the Greek philosopher Aristotle, is that it seeks to entertain and to instruct, giving its audience both pleasure and learning. Indeed, it should teach the audience through the medium of pleasure. Angela Carter's *Nights at the Circus*, with its range of unlikely or impossible characters, is certainly a swift-paced entertainment. Moreover, its subject is entertainment itself, set as it is in the backstage worlds of the music hall and the circus at the very end of the nineteenth century. Its central character, the bird-woman known as Fevvers, is an entertainer in this world. She is larger than life and twice as noisy, and is considerably more vulgar than the conventional novel heroine is supposed to be. Her perfume is too strong, her make-up too bright, her voice too loud, her hair and feathers dyed. She performs on the flying trapeze, and her act depends on keeping her audiences guessing: does this woman really have wings, or is she a spectacular fraud, and if she's a fraud, how does she do it? Fevvers is literally and figuratively 'a laugh'. From her first appearance where she speaks in a voice that clangs like dustbin lids, through her various adventures at home and abroad, to her laughter, spiralling like a tornado across the whole world, Fevvers is a figure of fun, living with laughter, and making others laugh too.

So much for entertainment: the instruction is of a different order. For although this is a comic novel, it is also a serious book which examines important philosophical questions about the nature of human existence. As we follow Fevvers's geographical journey, Angela Carter asks us also to undertake adventures in morality. *Nights at the Circus* has a lot of jokes and hilarity. But as we laugh, we are also asked to question the meaning of life. In taking Fevvers as her heroine, for example, Angela Carter is presenting us with a performer who uses every artificial means at her disposal to enhance her reputation and her appearance. Her centrality to the plot suggests that 'human nature' might just be one big performance too. Fevvers's femininity is an elaborate charade, a series of costume changes supplemented by the constant reapplication of make-up. What does it mean to be a woman in a culture that values a woman's attractiveness according to how well she fakes it? What can a woman's nature be in this world? By extension, what are the proper roles of masculinity, and what does it mean to be a man? What does being human mean? What does humanity owe to animals? Can we believe in people changing through time? What is love? The novel asks these questions, and proposes answers that unsettle the habitual thinking of cliché. Angela Carter's answers are never quite the ones that other kinds of novels might propose.

Nights at the Circus can be read as an example of the novel-genre of magic realism, a term developed to describe a narrative in which reality and fantasy elements are fused. There is certainly magic in *Nights at the Circus*. Fevvers's very existence as a woman with wings establishes the element of the fantastic from the outset. And yet Fevvers is also very 'real'. She is, for example, very preoccupied with the material elements of her existence: the food she eats, the champagne she drinks, the money she earns. There's an emphasis in her character on practical financial good sense. Moreover, for a 'heavenly body', she has an earthy sense of humour and a total disregard for the conventional proprieties around breaking wind. Her 'realness' sits uneasily with her position as a fantasy figure. Her publicity posters ask, 'Is she fact or fiction?', a question that might well be rewritten as 'is she real or is she magic?' The genre of magic realism will not allow us to answer that question by plumping for one alternative or the other. The answer is probably that she is both – fiction and fact, magic and real – and we are not allowed to see the join. The incursion of magic into reality, represented by Fevvers, suggests that we need to look anew at reality. Hers is a world in which nothing is quite what it seems. Angela Carter's novel thereby offers a challenge to its own audience. In the world beyond the circus – our world – we need to question our common-sense version of reality. In entertaining us, Fevvers unsettles us: being unsettled appears to be the prerequisite for learning the new ways of seeing the world in which she also instructs us.

PART TWO

SUMMARIES & COMMENTARIES

Nights at the Circus was first published by Chatto and Windus in 1984, and reissued a year later in paperback by Picador. It received favourable reviews which recognised the density of its narrative style, the strangeness of its imagination, the confidence of its vision, and the attractiveness of its heroine, and it won the James Tait Black Memorial Prize (1985). The book was largely responsible for a resurgence of interest in Angela Carter's writing. Angela Carter had been a novelist since the mid 1960s, and two of her earlier fictions (*The Magic Toyshop*, 1967, and *Several Perceptions*, 1968) had been prizewinners in their time, but her reputation amongst the critics had suffered during the 1970s. There are many reasons for this critical decline; but one significant explanation is perhaps that Angela Carter's works resist generic classification. Her books combine realism, politics, fantasy, science fiction, fairy tale, folk tale, the erotic and the Gothic, amongst others. They cannot be easily pigeon-holed by publishers aiming at a particular readership or by readers themselves. Across the whole of Angela Carter's writing, one never knows quite what to expect – and this tendency to upend the reader is particularly marked in *Nights at the Circus*. Fevvers is portrayed 'bums aloft' (p. 7) in one of her publicity posters; that might equally be the reader's undignified position.

The text referred to in this Note is the Vintage paperback edition published in 1994.

SYNOPSIS

Nights at the Circus is divided into three parts, 'London', 'Petersburg' and 'Siberia', each further divided into a number of chapters. It tells the life and picaresque adventures of a trapeze artiste named Fevvers, an anomaly of nature who was hatched from an egg in East London, and who developed wings at puberty.

The first section is set in London towards the end of the nineteenth century, in Fevvers's dressing room at the Alhambra. In the company of her adoptive mother, Lizzie, Fevvers is being interviewed by a young American journalist named Jack Walser whose ostensible intention is to explode Fevvers's reputation as a real woman who also has real wings. The whole of the first part of the novel involves Fevvers telling her life story to this sceptical audience with interruptions from Lizzie. She explains to Walser that she was found on the doorstep of a Whitechapel brothel in a basket amongst the eggshells from which she had hatched. She was brought up by the prostitutes, led by a one-eyed madam nicknamed Nelson, but largely in the care of Lizzie. The household did not exploit her in their sexual business, but used her to pose in *tableaux vivants* as the figure of Cupid, and later, as the Winged Victory, the goddess Nike. When Nelson died in a carriage accident the brothel was dispersed and Fevvers began to wander the world: at first she worked with Lizzie's family in an ice-cream parlour (Lizzie comes from Sicilian stock); then she became part of a disturbing freak show run by the infamous Madame Schreck in which clients came to gawp at, and have sex with, various wondrous women. Her sojourn at the Museum of Horrors ends when she is sold by Madame Schreck to a client named Christian Rosencreutz, who seeks to make a human sacrifice of her – she escapes by flying naked through his window. Since then, she has made her living in the music halls and nightclubs of Western Europe as a trapeze artist, which brings us to the present of the narrative. Walser is disturbed during the telling of the story to discover that time itself seems to have been altered by Fevvers's storytelling: the clock strikes midnight many times before morning comes. He is so fascinated by Fevvers that he goes next day to the offices of Colonel Kearney, an American impresario who plans to tour his circus in Russia and the Far East. Walser's plan is to join and spend some nights at the circus in pursuit of Fevvers and her story. He is engaged as a clown.

Part Two, 'Petersburg', is, as the title suggests, set in St Petersburg, where Colonel Kearney's circus has arrived at the Imperial State Circus. Walser, now disguised as a clown, is living in lodgings in Clown Alley, whilst Fevvers is put up at the best hotel. This, like the first part of the novel, is a very episodic narrative, largely told in the third person. It narrates the daily life of the circus, including how Walser is attacked by a tiger, how he becomes a human chicken in the clowns' act, how he rescues the abused Mignon from her terrible husband and places her under Fevvers's protection, how Mignon joins an Abyssinian Princess in the tiger act, how Fevvers is attacked by jealous Italian trapeze artists, how the troupe of Educated Apes liberate themselves from their contract and leave the circus, and how the stupid Strong Man begins the process of learning emotion and sensitivity. A central scene in this section is the descent into madness of the head clown, Buffo the Great. Before his last performance, he drinks himself into a frenzy, and during the Clowns' Christmas dinner sketch, where Walser plays the Human Chicken, he tries to kill the journalist. He is eventually overpowered, and dragged away to the madhouse. In this section, it starts to become clear that Walser is losing his scepticism and becoming increasingly attracted to Fevvers. At the end of the Petersburg section, Fevvers finds herself in extreme danger. She has agreed to go the house of a Grand Duke because he has promised her a diamond necklace. His motives, however, are far from honourable, and he seeks to entrap her in a miniature Fabergé egg. She magically escapes to the train which is now leaving to take the circus across Siberia to Japan.

In 'Siberia', the circus indeed reaches Siberia by train. But the train is blown up by outlaws seeking to enlist Fevvers's support in putting their case to the Tsar. The circus animals are killed in the aftermath of the explosion. The remnants of the circus, including Fevvers, now with a broken wing, Lizzie, Colonel Kearney, the clowns, the Princess and Mignon, and the Strong Man, are kidnapped by the bandits. Walser remains buried in the wreckage of the train. He has lost his memory and his mind in the explosion and ends up wandering the wastelands of Siberia. He is eventually 'rescued' by a Shaman from a remote tribe who believes him to be a spirit or a Shaman himself. He is initiated in the ways of the tribe, having completely forgotten who he really is. Fevvers and the rest of the circus, meanwhile, escape from their captivity in a freak whirlwind that carries the outlaws and the clowns away. They walk across the wilderness until they come upon a strange building in which a mad Maestro is in charge of a musical conservatoire. At the conservatoire, Mignon's singing and the Princess's playing enchant nature, and bring the tribespeople with whom Walser is living out from the woods. The tribe departs with Walser still in tow. Mignon, the Princess and the

Strong Man elect to remain at the conservatoire to pursue a career in music; Colonel Kearney and one remaining outlaw (an escaped anarchist) set out towards civilisation; and Fevvers and Lizzie decide to find Walser. They find him in the Shaman's village, and as the journalist starts to regain his mind, he and Fevvers go to bed together.

PART ONE: LONDON

CHAPTER 1   **We become acquainted with Fevvers through the eyes of Jack Walser as she begins to tell him her story**

It is almost midnight one night some time in late 1899. The novel opens at the Alhambra music hall in the dressing room of the world-famous bird-woman, Fevvers, trapeze artist *extraordinaire*. Fevvers, chaperoned by her dresser, Lizzie, is telling her story to an American journalist named Jack Walser, a sceptical man who believes that she is a fraud. Her dressing room is littered with the accoutrements of her profession. Her costumes and underwear are strewn about; the walls are papered with her publicity posters; the smell in the room – of perfume, greasepaint, hot bodies and fish – is overpowering and disorienting for Walser. It affects his ability to concentrate, and to maintain his objectivity.

Fevvers's narrative does not proceed in a straightforward way. She begins at the beginning, with the statement that she was 'Hatched out of a bloody great egg' (p. 7), but her story is punctuated by digression and apparent irrelevance. She talks and talks, letting slip scandalous information, such as the perverse sexual favours preferred by Henri de Toulouse-Lautrec who painted one of her publicity posters; and that her solid gold hairbrush is a gift from the Prince of Wales. The proliferation of details, most of them unprintable for a journalist in the late 1890s, confuses Walser, as do the champagne that they all drink, and the strong smell of the room.

In Fevvers's few silences, there are descriptions of Walser as a rather unfinished character, untouched by most of his experiences because of his journalistic objectivity. We enter his mind and sense his disorientation. He tries to reason with himself that what Fevvers claims to be is in fact physiologically impossible. He muses about whether she has a belly button; he considers the fact that wings are to birds what arms are to people, and that the possession of both wings and arms is therefore illogical. At the end of the chapter, however, he is no more sure of his grounds than he was at the beginning. And Fevvers, after many digressions, returns to her beginning again, restarting her story with the fact that she was 'Hatched'.

> This opening chapter works in a dual way. As Fevvers tells us her story, we are of course, becoming more informed about her and her life. At the same time, however, increased knowledge about her paradoxically produces increased confusion. The world Angela Carter presents us with is an intensely realistic one in which the material conditions of Fevvers's life – her clothes, make-up, furniture, food and drink, artificial scent and natural odour – are thrust to the forefront of the narrative. These details appear to be the markers of **verisimilitude**. But in the midst of all this solid and rather sordid reality, we are asked to believe the impossible: that Fevvers is a woman with wings. In encountering an ostensibly **realist** narrative with a fantastic central fact, the reader's expectations – like Walser's – are subverted.
>
> The central question of Fevvers's existence comes from her own publicity material: 'Is she fact or is she fiction?' This is impossible to answer because Fevvers is a performer. Her life depends on illusion and deception, from the peroxide she uses to dye her hair blonde, to the make-up she wears to disguise her real face, to the costumes she wears that disguise her real body ('her nakedness was certainly a stage illusion', p. 18). On the stage, she looks like an angel. Close to, she looks like a 'dray mare' (p. 12). Which is the real Fevvers? The question of reality and appearance is one of the key themes of the novel as a whole. Fevvers's effects are the effects of artifice. She performs even when playing herself. Her opening words, 'Lor' love you, sir!', are the words of a cockney from the music-hall stage rather than the words of any real Londoner. Her language is a kind of fake and should never quite be taken at face value. Walser, the sceptical journalist, is therefore an ideal audience for her. He is not inclined to believe in her, but he cannot help being overwhelmed by her performance, drugged in part by

champagne, in part by strong odours, and finally hypnotised by Fevvers's presence.

Another theme of the text that is signalled in this opening is that of the expectations of gender – what are the proper roles of masculinity and femininity? Fevvers is extremely vulgar. Her voice is loud, her language and manners coarse, her appetite huge, her smell is strong and her make-up is laid on with a trowel. These are not the attributes of proper femininity, whether at the end of the nineteenth century when the novel is set, or the end of the twentieth when the novel was written. If Fevvers performs one kind of gender, a parody of femininity, Walser is apparently a conspicuously manly man, performing the role of masculinity. He is a war correspondent and 'would have called himself a "man of action"' (p. 10). But he is untouched by his experience because he lacks self-consciousness. As a woman and a performer, Fevvers is acutely self-aware at all times, always watching for the effect that her performance has on others. This is the element of character that Walser lacks at the outset. The novel charts, among other things, his achievement of self-consciousness.

Helen of Troy Helen of Troy was hatched from an egg; her mother Leda had sexual congress with Zeus, king of the gods, who descended from heaven in the form of a swan

Bow Bells to have been born within earshot of Bow Bells is the traditional definition of a cockney

aerialiste trapeze artist (French)

steatopygous large buttocked

as the old saint said Pope Gregory (*c.*540–604). He sent missionaries to convert the English because they were so beautiful: 'not Angles but Angels'

some Frog dwarf Henri de Toulouse-Lautrec (1864–1901), a French painter of notoriously short stature, was famous for his depictions of the backstage life of music-hall dancers and singers, and for designing their publicity posters

Dan Leno music-hall comedian of the late nineteenth century (1860–1904)

this Helen launched a thousand quips c.f. Christopher Marlowe's *Doctor Faustus* (1604), in which Faustus looks at Helen and says: 'Is this the face that launched a thousand ships?'

picaresque from the Spanish word *picaro*, rogue, picaresque usually describes a narrative in which a low-life character takes to the road and has adventures

Call him Ishmael the first words of Herman Melville's 1851 novel *Moby Dick* are 'Call me Ishmael.'

objet trouvé found object (French)

bonhomerie – bonnefemmerie literally 'good man-ness – good woman-ness' (French – *bonhomie*, meaning geniality). 'Bonnefemmerie' is Angela Carter's own coinage

post-impressionists a late-nineteenth-century school of French art that developed from the Impressionist school of the 1870s

Willy ... Colette Sidonie-Gabrielle Colette (1873–1954), French novelist whose first husband, Willy, appropriated her work and published it under his name

Alfred Jarry (1873–1907) French playwright and notorious alcoholic and rabble rouser

Sophie Fevvers's real name is derived from the Greek for 'wisdom'

Toujours, Toulouse signature of Toulouse-Lautrec: 'forever, Toulouse' (French)

'Only a bird in a gilded cage' late-nineteenth-century music-hall song

'The Ride of the Valkyries' from the *Ring* cycle of operas by Richard Wagner (1813–83). In Scandinavian mythology, the Valkyries were the winged angels of fate who rode into battle with drawn swords and decided who would live or die

cache-sexe literally 'concealer of sex' (French); Fevvers wears a body stocking with strategically placed sequins to disguise her breasts and pubic region

Rubenesque form the painter Rubens (1577–1640) is famous for having painted women with very fleshy bodies

Valhalla in Scandinavian mythology, the palace in which the souls of dead heroes feasted

in utero in the womb (Latin)

oviparous species species that reproduce by the means of eggs, especially birds

CHAPTER *2*   Fevvers describes her life at Nelson's brothel and
her experiments with flight. After Nelson's death,
the brothel breaks up, and the ex-whores go their
separate ways

Interrupted by a brief interlude for a gargantuan and unladylike meal,
Fevvers begins to tell her story again. She was abandoned as a baby
amongst her eggshells at the door of a brothel in London's East End.
Fevvers was brought up by the prostitutes who worked there, including
Lizzie – the dresser and her adoptive mother – and the brothel's madam,
nicknamed Nelson because she had only one eye. In the brothel, as a
small child, she played the figure of Cupid, a role she fulfilled through her
girlhood until puberty, when her wings suddenly appeared. Thereafter
she played the goddess Nike, the Winged Victory.

As time went on, Fevvers realised that with wings she ought to be
able to fly. She narrates her experiments with flight, including her
disastrous launch from a large marble fireplace, when she clattered to the
ground and broke her nose. After that, she decided to be more scientific
in her approach, and studied the flight of real birds. She learned that she
would have to *make* herself fly, and launched herself from the brothel's
roof. After a few scares, she mastered the basics of flight. Walser, lulled
into an almost hypnotic state by Fevvers's storytelling, hears Big Ben
strike midnight.

Fevvers describes the working life of the brothel. Her own role as
Winged Victory was slightly difficult to achieve, since the Greek statue
on which the figure is based has no arms. Ma Nelson solved the problem
of what to do with her hands by giving her a sword. When the girls were
not working, during the day, they practised music and typewriting, or
spent time reading and pursuing other intellectual activities. Fevvers
passed the days in Nelson's library, studying aerodynamics, or at London
Zoo, watching the cranes and the storks. In a pause while Lizzie makes
tea, Big Ben again strikes midnight, and Walser realises the extent of his
own disorientation. He has become the prisoner of Fevvers's voice.

After tea, the story picks up with Nelson's sudden death: she was
run over. This signals the end of the Whitechapel brothel, and the break-
up of the family of whores. Nelson's brother, a clergyman, threw them
out. The women dispersed to different lives: two to set up a boarding

house in Brighton, two to establish a typing agency, one, Jenny, to marry a lord who died of the *bombe surprise* at their wedding reception and left his sorrowing widow a very wealthy woman. She then married an American millionaire. The last woman went into show business. And Fevvers and Lizzie went back to Lizzie's family to join the ice-cream making business: *bombe surprise* is a speciality of the house. They all took a souvenir from Nelson's brothel: Lizzie took a French clock (though it does not work) without which she never leaves home and Fevvers took Nelson's sword for reasons of 'sentiment and self-protection' (p. 48). As they left, they set the house on fire.

As the narrative of Fevvers's early life unfolds, with interruptions for meat pie, eel gravy and mash, for more champagne and for tea, Fevvers's own character emerges. Her appetite is enormous – no tiny, ladylike portions for her, but a huge feast. Her table manners also leave much to be desired, with peas eaten from her knife, gravy sloshed about and wind unrestrainedly released. It is almost as though Fevvers is testing Walser's stomach for her story by testing his stomach for her manners: her behaviour is so different from what is usually expected from nice women.

In this chapter, too, Fevvers demonstrates an ironic attitude to life. Her playing of Cupid, the god of love, amongst the prostitutes is one example. Another is the fact that in telling the story of Nelson's brothel, she reduces one of the great heroes of the British Empire to a figure of fun: to an old whore who dresses in men's clothing, and who lost her eye in a decidedly unheroic encounter with a sailor in the year of the Great Exhibition (pp. 22–3). The telling of Nelson's story is a masterpiece of comic timing, in which first her name is given, then her occupation, then the story of the lost eye. As more information is released – for example, that Ma Nelson owned valuable pictures, and that she was sufficiently educated to have a well-argued philosophy – Walser is forced to ask himself whether he believes in 'a one-eyed, metaphysical madame, in Whitechapel, in possession of a Titian' (p. 28). Only four pages later do we learn that 'due to her soubriquet, or nickname, [Nelson] always dressed in the full dress uniform of an Admiral of the Fleet' (p. 32). The piling up of irreverent detail on the name of Horatio

Nelson depends for its effect on the idea that Nelson is a significant figure, a man to be admired. Ma Nelson's existence, and her far from glorious death, having slipped on 'skin of a fruit or dog turd' (p. 43) effectively debunks the idea of heroism that Nelson is supposed to have represented. Moreover, Lizzie and Fevvers are aware of this in their telling of the story. As Lizzie comments, in a reference to Admiral Nelson's deathbed scene on board ship: 'No chance for even so much as a "Kiss me, Hardy", nor any tender final words like that' (p. 43).

From the first chapter, the theme of the illusionary nature of experience is developed further. Fevvers admits to Walser that she dyes her hair and her feathers to heighten the effect of her appearance. In itself, that's no surprise. But this notion of illusion is developed in different ways. In describing the life of the brothel, for example, Fevvers implicitly draws a comparison between the selling of women's bodies in prostitution, and her own more recent, more respectable career on the stage. She tells Walser: 'we knew we only sold the *simulacra* of sexual pleasure (p. 39). The brothel, like the stage, is a place that is filled with deceptions and forgery: there's no sincerity or authenticity about the transactions in either space. This is made all the clearer when, after Nelson's death, the women decide to open the curtains and let in the light: 'The luxury of that place had been nothing but illusion, created by the candles of midnight, and, in the dawn, all was sere, worn-out decay' (p. 49). The illusion is what they sell to their clients, but they have to avoid being trapped in it, avoid believing in the illusion they have made. The whores leave to go to new more realistic lives in commerce and in marriage.

Another important theme that is developed in this chapter is that of time. It is in this chapter that Lizzie's clock, rescued from Ma Nelson's house, first makes its appearance. Given that the scene is already set at a highly significant time (near midnight towards the end of the nineteenth century) the appearance of the clock from under a pair of Fevvers's discarded knickers is clearly meant to be more than just local decoration, particularly since it is clock time that so confuses Walser as the process of his disorientation continues. He hears the bells of Big Ben strike midnight three times in this chapter, heralding a new day. Clock time is presumably one of the objective measures by which he understands his world. When clock time can no longer be relied on, he loses his bearings. Lizzie's clock, of course, does not work. It always tells midnight or midday, and so is accurate twice a day. Midnight is traditionally the witching hour, and Walser is being bewitched, it would seem, by a clock that holds time still. In Ma Nelson's words, the clock showed 'the dead centre of the day or night, the shadowless hour, the hour of vision and revelation, the still hour in the centre of the storm of time' (p. 29). That same clock, now covered with Fevvers's hastily removed drawers, presides over the telling of Fevvers's life to Walser, holding him still.

Fujiyama Mount Fujiyama is the highest mountain in Japan

Nelson Ma Nelson is named after Horatio Nelson (1758–1805), British naval hero who famously lost one eye in battle

Great Exhibition held at the Crystal Palace in 1851, the Great Exhibition was a showcase for British and Imperial industry and culture

tableau vivant literally, 'living picture' (French), pose

Winged Victory Nike, or the Winged Victory of Samothrace, is a famous Ancient Greek statue portraying a winged woman. The statue is damaged and has no head, and it was designed without arms

Age of Reason more or less, the eighteenth century, a period during which Enlightenment thinkers were convinced that reason could solve the problems of the world and rid it of superstition, barbarity and ignorance

Vesta Roman goddess of home and hearth, who tended the fire in the house

where burns the pyre of the Arabian bird the Arabian bird is the mythical phoenix that dies on its funeral pyre, and then resurrects from its own ashes

Venetian school Renaissance painters of the fifteenth and sixteenth centuries

Titian (1488–1576), painter of the Venetian school

Svengali the evil impresario who moulds a working-class singer into a star in George du Maurier's 1894 novel *Trilby*

Bokhara carpet luxurious Arabian carpet

Chinese boxes box within a box within a box etc., hence an image of infinity

Lucifer the name of Satan, the fallen angel, before he was driven from heaven for his pride; the name literally means 'light-bearer'

Germoline the brand name of a soothing antiseptic cream still sold today

Icarus in Greek mythology, Icarus had wings made by his father from wax. But he flew too close to the sun, the wax melted, he tumbled into the sea and was drowned

Old Father Thames this description of the Thames is a play on the personification of Time, Old Father Time

Brobdingnagian Brobdingnag is the land of giants encountered by Gulliver in Jonathan Swift's *Gulliver's Travels* (1726)

hubris overweening pride – the pride that traditionally comes before a fall in Greek tragedy; the tragic flaw of a mythological hero

a staff with which to conduct her revels – her wand, like Prospero's in Shakespeare's play *The Tempest*, Prospero is a wizard-figure with a magic staff. Towards the end of the play, he tells the audience that 'Our revels now are ended', and that everything they have seen before presented before them is a kind of dream (Act IV, Scene 1)

Baudelaire Charles Baudelaire (1821–1867), French poet famous for highly sexualised subject matter

simulacra deceptive substitutes (from Latin, singular form = *simulacrum*)

'*luxe, calme, volupté*' quotation from Baudelaire's poem 'Invitation au voyage' (Invitation to the voyage); 'luxuriousness, calm, sensuality'

Scheherazade the narrator of the *Thousand and One Nights* cycle of stories

travestie dressing in drag (French)

Roaring Forties and Furious Fifties the Roaring Forties are strong winds found in the Southern hemisphere at around latitude 40°; the Furious Fifties appear to be Fevvers's own coinage

Cockney sparrow allusion to Edith Piaf (1915–63), French singer, whose career began on the streets. Piaf's name derives from the Parisian slang word for sparrow. The designation 'cockney sparrow' is ironic in Fevvers's case, since she is anything but diminutive

a siren's in Greek mythology, the singing of the sirens was fatal since it made the hearer forget everything, including food, so he would starve to death

growler a four-wheeled horse-drawn cab

bombe surprise literally 'surprise bomb' (French), an ice-cream dessert

a gentleman from Chicago who makes sewing machines possibly a veiled reference to Isaac Merritt Singer (1811–75), inventor of the sewing machine

cassata Italian ice cream containing candied fruit and nuts

il mio papa my father (Italian)

CHAPTER 3   **Fevvers and Lizzie make and sell ice cream, but business is not good, and Fevvers joins Madame Schreck's museum of female monsters**

Despite her earlier enormous meal, Fevvers is again hungry, and Lizzie goes to find a bacon sandwich. Alone with Fevvers, Walser becomes panicky, and tries to leave the room, pleading a call of nature. But he is not allowed to leave, and has to relieve himself in the chamber pot behind the screen in the dressing room. When he has done, and Lizzie is on her way back with more tea, Big Ben strikes midnight again, and Fevvers restarts her narrative. After the brothel, she and Lizzie went to live in Battersea where they made and sold ice cream in the family business. But business took a turn for the worse. When things were at their lowest ebb, a strange veiled woman arrived suddenly one day with a proposition that Fevvers should join a freak show. The woman was called Madame Schreck, a name that Walser has heard before, and it makes him shudder. Had it not been for the catalogue of disasters that befell the ice-cream-making family, Fevvers would never have gone near Madame Schreck. But in dire financial straits, she secretly left the house for a new and sinister career.

In Chapter 2 Fevvers had argued passionately that prostitution is caused by material considerations, not sensual pleasure. 'No woman would turn her belly to the trade unless pricked by economic necessity, sir,' she tells Walser (p. 39). Chapter 3 demonstrates that this has been Fevvers's own spur to action. Life at the Battersea ice-cream parlour should have been idyllic. But circumstances conspire against happiness. This chapter elaborates one of the novel's political themes – that poverty takes away your choices. Fevvers 'chooses' a dubious career in Madame Schreck's museum of horrors because she has no real choice in the face of 'an accumulation of those unpredictable catastrophes that precipitate poor folk such as we into the abyss of poverty through no fault of their own' (p. 56). Fevvers's appetite and material greed – at the beginning of the chapter she is again hungry and sends Lizzie out for bacon sandwiches – are the legacy of her original poverty.

Montgolfier Jean-Joseph and Jacques-Etienne Montgolfier, inventors of the hot-air balloon (1782)
Crookback Dick ... Malvolio's yellow stockings Crookback Dick is the hero/villain of Shakespeare's *Richard III*; Malvolio is the butt of many jokes in *Twelfth Night*
Marriage of Figaro 1786 opera by Wolfgang Amadeus Mozart (1756–91)

CHAPTER 4 **Fevvers describes her stay at Madame Schreck's museum and her eventual departure**

Nelson's brothel had been an honourable house, but Madame Schreck's museum was a grimmer proposition. The museum was in Kensington (a smart area of London), though it was anything but respectable. Fevvers was admitted to the house by Madame Schreck's 'butler', a man with no mouth, named Toussaint. (As an aside, Fevvers tells Walser that following her success in show business she paid for a famous Harley Street doctor to operate on Toussaint to give him a mouth, and gives him a checkable fact, the date of the edition of *The Lancet* in which the operation is described.) Madame Schreck was a deathly figure, so thin that she had once made her living as a 'Living Skeleton' in sideshows. The other inmates were 'prodigies of nature' (p. 59), women, like Fevvers, who had been born with remarkable and monstrous physical attributes.

The house was really a brothel. Clients arrived, dressed up in their fantasy choice of costume, and were conducted to a vault beneath the house, where the women stood or lay in stone niches behind curtains, while Toussaint played atmospheric music on an old harmonium. The clients might choose to sleep with any of the women with the exception of Fevvers, who guarded her virginity, and of the Sleeping Beauty, whose speciality lay in the fact that she could not wake up. For this work, the women were to be paid around ten pounds per week, but in fact they saw none of the profit.

Each woman had her tragic story. The Sleeping Beauty was a curate's daughter who had fallen into lethargy at the onset of puberty. Her parents had passed her into Madame Schreck's care because she had promised to bring their daughter to the best doctors. The Sleeping Beauty woke for only a few moments a day, to eat and empty her bowels. Otherwise she was completely still, except that her sleep was filled with troublesome dreams.

The Wiltshire Wonder was only three feet high, the offspring of a country wench and the King of the Fairies, conceived in a mystical mound in Wiltshire. As a child, she had made her living in fairgrounds, but her mother had sold her to a pastry chef, who used her as a surprise centrepiece, required to leap out of birthday cakes for rich children. At one party she had surfaced prematurely, setting herself and the table alight with the birthday candles in the process. Luckily, one small girl had wrapped her in a napkin to put out the flames, and had fallen so in love with the midget that she was adopted by the little girl's family. Unfortunately the Wiltshire Wonder had inherited her mother's lusty nature and, one night at the pantomime, had run away with the dwarves from a production of *Snow White*. Although she was still a child, the dwarves had sexually abused her, passing her from one to another. She had been abandoned penniless in Berlin, where Madame Schreck had picked her up.

Fanny Four-Eyes appeared quite ordinary at first sight, but she had eyes where she should have had nipples. Cobwebs was a girl with cobwebs on her face, and she could never be made to laugh or smile. Albert/Albertina was a hermaphrodite, and consequently Madame Schreck could charge high fees for her (or his?) sexual services since s/he could pleasure clients in two distinct ways. Fevvers's own role in the brothel was to stand guard over the Sleeping Beauty, playing the role of an Angel of Death. Sleeping Beauty's health was so precarious that she could not participate in sexual activity.

One day, a new client arrived, and became obsessed with Fevvers. He came to the 'museum' regularly to see her, and then Fevvers was summoned into Madame Schreck's presence to be told that he had made an offer for her. The man's name was Christian Rosencreutz. Fevvers is suspicious about the arrangement, and pretty sure that Madame Schreck will try to cheat her out of her fee. She picks her up and hangs her from a curtain pole high in the room in order to ensure that she gets her proper share of the money from Madame Schreck's open safe. But just as Fevvers is about to collect her gold, a loud knocking is heard throughout the house, and two large men capture Fevvers in a net and take her away in a horse and carriage.

This chapter is one of the places in which the novel's genre is uncertain. Fevvers's narrative is usually good-humoured and jokey, milking the comic potential of what she describes. But Madame Schreck's museum of horrors is no laughing matter. When Fevvers mentioned her name in the previous chapter, Walser shivered: he had already heard of her 'vague rumours in men's clubs, over brandy and cigars, the name never accompanied by guffaws, leers, nudges in the ribs, but by bare, hinted whispers of the profoundly strange, of curious revelations that greeted you behind Our Lady of Terror's triple-locked doors' (p. 55). Laughter and slightly coarse innuendo are generally regarded in the novel as proper responses to sex; but sometimes sexual activity is just not funny.

In Madame Schreck's museum we move from the world of comedy to the world of the Gothic, a realm of horror not humour. Angela Carter's narrator and heroine are both highly tolerant of sexual activity in general. At Nelson's brothel, Fevvers comments, 'the pleasures of the flesh were, at bottom, splendid'. Madame Schreck, however, 'catered for those who were troubled in their souls' (p. 57). This is a much nastier, more exploitative kind of prostitution, not least because the whores themselves never see the profits from the sales. But also, of course, the museum is creepy because the attractions of the house are to do with the freakish nature of its occupants. It is a nightmarish space.

Angela Carter's point, however, is not just to shock the reader or Walser with a story of depravity. Later in the text we will come across the story of Mignon, a German orphan. Her degraded life is a more ordinary story, but it has much in common with various prodigies of nature in the museum. Angela Carter was certainly writing from a feminist perspective: the catalogues of whores and victims (and of whores *as* victims) imply that the novel views male attitudes to women as generally exploitative.

At the end of the chapter, when Fevvers is captured by Rosencreutz's silent henchmen, another scene is prefigured. As she admits herself, 'The gold it was that trapped me, for I could not bear to cast aside that glinting pile of treasure and flee' (p. 72). At the end of the 'Petersburg' section a similar situation will see Fevvers again in peril because of her greed for material things. She is a voracious figure, and her voracity is sometimes her downfall.

Toussaint French for All Saints' Day (1 November), the day after Halloween

Kyrie *Kyrie eleison* are the Greek words for 'Lord have mercy' from the Christian service

Virgil ... Dante in Dante's *Divine Comedy* (c.1321), the poet is led to the regions of Hell and Purgatory by the Roman poet Virgil

patisseur pastry-maker (French)

bonne bouche literally 'good mouth' (French), meaning titbit, sweetmeat

this rag-and-bone shop of the heart quotation from W.B. Yeats's poem 'The Circus Animals' Desertion' (1939)

'What a wonderful piece of work is man' a misquotation from *Hamlet*, II.2.303–4. The line actually reads: 'What a piece of work is a man'

Christian Rosencreutz an assumed name (Fevvers will later tells Walser his real name, p. 78). A real Christian Rosencreutz existed in history (1378–1484): he was an occultist who claimed to possess spiritual powers derived from travels in the East. Many occult writings are attributed to him, and he is credited with founding the Order of the Rosy Cross , an occult sect. Fevvers's Christian Rosencreutz borrows the name partly for disguise, but also because he is a follower of the Rosicrucian system

CHAPTER 5   **Fevvers's encounter with and escape from Christian Rosencreutz, and the end of Madame Schreck's museum**

Fevvers and her kidnappers pull up in front of an incongruously brand new fake-Gothic medieval mansion, where Mr 'Rosencreutz' awaits them. He welcomes Fevvers to his home, and sends her off to the bathroom to wash. While she is in the bathroom, her host sets Fevvers a riddle: she is to come out of the room 'neither naked nor clothed' (p. 76); she covers her body with her abundant hair and secures Nelson's sword into this arrangement. She and Rosencreutz then go downstairs for a meal, and while Fevvers eats with her usual enthusiasm, Rosencreutz expounds his philosophy. He believes in the essential evil of the female sexual organ, and in the potency of the phallus (round his neck he wears a solid gold medallion engraved with a phallus). His philosophy is a mish-mash of systems – Hindu, Jewish, Christian, classical, pagan, folklore and Arthurian legend – but in his rendition of these ideas, they all focus on the necessity of annihilating the female by the power of the male phallus: that is the secret of eternal life. (In an aside, Fevvers tells Walser that Rosencreutz is in fact an MP who campaigns against rights for women. She writes his name in Walser's notebook and scandalises him.) Rosencreutz talks all night, but just as the sun rises, he opens the window in readiness for his ceremony.

Fevvers is required to lie on her back on an altar; she assumes that her host's purpose is sexual. But when his cloak falls open she notices that he has a sword concealed underneath, and realises that she is about to become a human sacrifice. She leaps up from the altar and brandishes her own sword before escaping through the open window. Rosencreutz tries to stop her, and wounds her foot (she shows Walser the scar as evidence), but she gets away. She navigates back to London by the railway line. When she gets back to Battersea, she finds that her own bed with Lizzie is occupied by the Sleeping Beauty.

Now Lizzie takes up the story reading from Toussaint's written testimony. The Battersea house is full of refugees from Madame Schreck's. Toussaint had tried to follow the carriage that had kidnapped Fevvers, but had lost sight of it. When he returned to the house, Madame Schreck, still hanging from the curtain pole where Fevvers had deposited her, appeared to be dead. Toussaint lifted her down and discovered that her clothes contained only a sprinkling of dust. He could not go to the police with the story of Fevvers's disappearance and of Madame Schreck's death: no one would believe him. At this point, Fanny took charge. She went to the still-open safe and took from it what each of the museum's employees was owed in wages, including a share for Fevvers. Then they all escaped to Lizzie's home in Battersea which was the only friendly address they had ever heard of.

The inmates of the museum of horrors dispersed. The Wiltshire Wonder returned to her adoptive parents who welcomed her back into the bosom of their family. Albert/Albertina became a ladies' maid. Fanny used her savings from Madame Schreck's to establish an orphanage. And Cobwebs trained as an artist in chiaroscuro, since she already saw the world in terms of exaggerated shade and light. The Sleeping Beauty lives still in Battersea, sleeps more and more, and is still dreaming. Her dream is of 'the coming century', and it is a very troubled dream: 'And, oh God ... how frequently she weeps!' (p. 86). At that, Fevvers falls silent and in the distance Big Ben strikes six. This is the end of the interview. Briskly, Fevvers tells how Esmeralda (one of Nelson's whores) suggested a career on the flying trapeze as a good job for a winged woman: 'The rest is history' (p. 87). Fevvers has triumphed in all the major cities of Europe, and has just been approached by an American circus owner to tour St Petersburg, the Far East and the United States.

Fevvers and Lizzie set out to walk home. At Westminster Bridge, Walser bids them farewell. Later that morning, he drops into his newspaper office and announces that he is tired of being a war correspondent. He suggests instead that he sign up, incognito, for Captain Kearney's tour of Russia, and join Fevvers to report on her trip to the East. He invites his editor to 'spend a few nights at the circus' (p. 91).

The house at which Fevvers arrives is a proper setting for the confusions of its owner in this chapter. Christian Rosencreutz – not his real name, of course – has assimilated lots of different belief systems to his own purpose. His house is itself anomalous: made to look like one thing, while in fact being something else. Again, the theme of reality and illusion comes to the fore. In this case the house has been designed to look old, but is in fact new. Through a deathly congress with Fevvers, Rosencreutz seeks to make himself new again: to defy death. On the one hand, his views about women and death appear extreme and silly. But the juxtaposition of his occult beliefs with the detail that he is in fact an MP, a powerful man, with highly misogynistic views is very significant:

> I saw in the paper only yesterday how he gives the most impressive speech in the House on the subject of Votes for Women. Which he is against. On account of how women are of a different soul-substance from men, cut from a different bolt of spirit cloth, and altogether too pure and rarefied to be bothering their pretty little heads with things of *this* world, such as the Irish question and the Boer War. (pp. 78–9)

The idea that women are spiritually different from men is a fairly precise mirror of the kinds of things that male MPs were indeed saying to justify not granting female suffrage in around 1899. Rosencreutz's batty occult ideas about the fatality of the female sex organ and his wearing of the winged phallus, symbol of masculine supremacy, are in a direct line from the kind of male thinking that said that women should not vote, the narrative suggests. Like the house, which is new but looks old, Rosencreutz's ideas in the House of Commons are just the old misogynies cloaked in new language.

Just at the moment when Christian Rosencreutz is planning to make Fevvers into a human sacrifice she turns on him with Nelson's sword: 'He fell back, babbling, unfair, unfair ... he'd not thought the angel would come armed,' Fevvers says (p. 83). This chapter in general, and that comment in particular, elucidates one of the central themes of the novel, the idea that the bird-woman is a symbol, an embodiment of other people's desires. In his perverse imaginings, Rosencreutz has transformed Fevvers into the object of his own desire. He believes her to be the Angel of Death whose own death will grant him eternal life. He forgets that she has a subjectivity of her own. This is one of Fevvers's consistent problems throughout the text. As a performer it is her job to embody the desires of her audience; but when she leaves the stage her performing persona and her real personality are too often mixed up by those around her. Her power comes from her ability to resist other people's expectations of her, to be more than a symbol. In this case her resistance stops her from being killed. Her escape here prefigures her escape from the Grand Duke at the end of Part Two. Her escapes are assertions of her own individuality in the face of conventionalised expectations of femininity.

Like the break-up of Nelson's brothel, the break-up of Madame Schreck's little empire is accompanied by a detailed resumé of the fates of the inmates. This is a repeating structure in the novel: Fevvers's narrative is like gossip, and she is always interested in the people she has met, and in what has happened to them later. This structure will be seen again in a different form in the Siberian section of the novel, where the endings are less clear-cut. Narratives that resemble gossip are very seductive. The hearer wants to hear more. Walser has been dragged into Fevvers's story as if he has been seduced by her – as indeed he will be. Her performance as 'the artiste being interviewed' is sexy.

Azrael, Azrail, Ashriel, Azriel, Azaril, Gabriel names of angels associated with death in Christian, Islamic and earlier belief systems

Proserpine in Roman mythology, the bride of Pluto, kidnapped to the Underworld against her will

Mysterium Baphometis Revelatum literally, The Mysteries of Baphomet Revealed (Latin). Bap or Baphomet was an idol or symbol for a demon which occult sects like the Templars were reputed to use in their rituals

Lady Godiva Lady Godiva (d. c.1080) is supposed to have ridden naked through the streets of Coventry in protest against her husband's imposition of high taxes on the townsfolk. She protected her modesty with her hair

Honi soit qui mal y pense ... Yoni soit qui mal y pense literally, 'Evil be to he that thinks it' (medieval French), which Rosencreutz adapts to say that the female sex organ (Yoni) is the fount of evil

This is some kind of heretical possibly Manichean version of neo-Platonic Rosicrucianism ... Manicheanism is a religious system from the third century AD, the central tenet of which was that good and evil were a duality that could never be resolved in favour of good. Neo-Platonism refers to revivals of the ideas of Plato who had argued that what we take to be real is in fact illusory. The Rosicrucians were an occult sect associated with alchemy and – to Christians – blasphemy since they used the cross in their rituals. Rosencreutz's philosophy is based on incompatible systems

Flora; Azrael; Venus Pandemos! Flora was the Roman goddess of the flowers; Azrael, the Angel of Death; Venus Pandemos means Venus (Roman goddess of love) of all the people

heave ho and up he rises rewriting of a line from the traditional sea shanty 'What shall we do with a drunken sailor?' The line is usually, 'heave ho and up *she* rises', referring to the ship's anchor being pulled up by the ship's crew, but in this case Fevvers is making a vulgar joke about a male erection

erberus usually spelled 'erebus', one of the caves of hell

maenad in Greek mythology, a female follower of the god of wine, Bacchus; the Maenads are frenzied, presumably as the result of drink

Irish question and the Boer War both burning new issues in 1899. The Irish question concerned Irish home rule; the Boer War was an Imperialist conflict in South Africa (1899–1902). Fevvers and Lizzie's left-wing politics would make them sympathetic to Irish home rule and antipathetic to the Boer War

Artephius alchemist whose twelfth-century text *The Secret Book* describes a recipe for the philosopher's stone

King David ... Abishag the Shulamite when King David grew old, his servants sent out for a young virgin to sleep with him so that he would 'get heat'. Abishag the Shulamite (or, more usually, Shunammite) was the chosen virgin but their relationship was not consummated. See 1 Kings I:1–4

Nine Worthies heroes of Renaissance thought, including three Jews (David amongst them), three Christians and three pagans

Signor Guardi possibly a reference to Italian painter Francesco Guardi (1712–93), though this painter is not usually associated with occult practices or extreme longevity

Arioriph ... Achamatoth possibly invented names for deities

Johnny-come-quickly a vulgar play on the phrase 'Johnny-come-lately', meaning late arrival or upstart. In this case the phrase implies that Mr Rosencreutz's sexual prowess leaves much to be desired

rejuvenatrix female form of rejuvenator

Fructifying disc the sun

elixum vitae elixir of life (Latin)

chiaroscuro a painting technique that makes exaggerated use of light and shade

of stars and stripes, the jolly Old Glory itself the United States flag. The Old Glory is another popular name for the stars and stripes, coined around 1831

orts refuse, rubbish (medieval English)

prolegomena introduction

PART TWO: PETERSBURG

CHAPTER 1   Walser is hired as a clown in Colonel Kearney's circus

In a kitchen in the backstreets of Petersburg an old woman is heating a samovar. She is also trying to tell her grandson, Ivan, a story about a pig who went to Petersburg. She is exhausted, and the story will never be told. In another part of the same house, Walser, dressed as a clown, is writing an article about Petersburg which exaggerates its beauty. As the samovar finally boils Walser pauses in his narrative of the city, and the baboushka ends her story of the pig: a wolf eats him. The narrative explains how Walser has come there.

Colonel Kearney had come to Petersburg with his own pig to make money. His pig is named Sybil, an intelligent sow who can spell out her views using alphabet cards. When Walser had visited Kearney in London to try to join the imperial tour, it was the pig who settled his fate. Kearney had interviewed Walser over several bottles of bourbon. Sybil had nodded when asked if Walser should be engaged to join the circus, and had spelled out the word 'clown' when asked what his role should be.

So Walser is now in Petersburg, working as a journalist, dressed as a clown. When he has drunk his tea, he ends his report, and bribes Ivan to take it to the British Embassy to be sent to London in a diplomatic bag. His experience of Petersburg is very far from the beautiful city that he has described: he lives in the mean streets among syphilitic whores and drunks and vomit and dead dogs.

> This is a chapter in which little actually happens. Rather it establishes an unfamiliar atmosphere. London is a known space; but St Petersburg is exotic and different, and has the effect of defamiliarisation. The chapter is built on the contrast between the real, sordid, poverty-stricken life of the city, and the dreams that the city inspires in those who do not really know it. The baboushka's abortive attempt to tell Ivan a story about a pig is juxtaposed with Walser's lyrical prose about the city to highlight the ways in which Walser's version of the city is a distortion of its reality: the theme of illusion and truth reappears here in a different guise. The baboushka's story is very sparse, consisting of only one sentence, and that expressed in very plain language. Elsewhere in the house, Walser's writing has become uncharacteristically purple prose:
>
> Russia is a sphinx; St Petersburg, the beautiful smile of her face. Petersburg, loveliest of all hallucinations, the shimmering mirage in the Northern wilderness glimpsed for a breathless second between black forest and the frozen sea.
>
> Within the city, the sweet geometry of every prospect; outside, limitless Russia and the approaching storm. (p. 96)
>
> This style of writing is highly significant. Walser is a journalist, a dealer in objectivity and fact expressed in simple prose. As the

narrative comments: 'The city precipitated him towards hyperbole; never before had he bandied about so many adjectives' (p. 98). Here, however, disguised as a clown, he appears to be under the sway of a powerful illusion, seeing not what is there (the poverty, the dirt, the disease), but a romanticised dreamscape. Disguised as a clown rather than dressed as a journalist, he has become part of a fantasy that he does not control. He experiences 'the freedom that lies behind the mask' (p. 103). But it is a dangerous freedom because it will lead to his 'very self, as he had known it' being taken from him. This writing-down of illusions, therefore, prefigures what will happen to Walser in the rest of the novel: his eventual loss of all sense of objective reality when he loses his memory after the Siberian explosion. The explosion completes the process of disorientation and defamiliarisation that began with his enchantment with Fevvers and continues with his response to Russia.

In this chapter, we also get our first glimpse of the American impresario, Colonel Kearney, possibly a satirised version of the real American circus owner, Phineas T. Barnum (1810–91). Kearney is a caricature of a particular kind of American show-business capitalist. His costume, made up of the American flag and dollar signs, signals both hubristic patriotism and phenomenal greed. His dream of taking elephants across the tundra, in emulation of Hannibal – indeed, he believes that he will outdo the Carthaginian hero – is the symptom of the overweening pride that comes before a fall in the conventions of tragedy. Colonel Kearney, though, is a mock heroic figure, a character who demonstrates that the world we live in is resolutely not a heroic place despite his own heroic pretensions. 'What a visionary he was!', the narrative comments ironically (p. 103), since his vision is primarily to do with profits and dollar signs, rather than anything of real value. One aspect of Kearney that points to his debased vision is his reliance on the wisdom of Sybil the pig, another mock heroic figure. In the world of the novel the mythological sibyls, prophets and oracles from Greek mythology, have been replaced by a porker in a ruff who makes her prophecies on greasy alphabet cards. This is not a world fit for heroes to inhabit. Attempts at heroism generally end in comic failure, as Walser is soon to discover.

baboushka grandmother, old woman, named after the traditional headscarf of the peasant woman (Russian, usually spelled 'babushka')

Martha ... Mary the sisters of Lazarus, Martha and Mary are diametrically opposed figures. While Martha toils in the house and kitchen to make Christ welcome, Mary merely sits at his feet and listens to him. See the Bible, Luke 10:38–42

St. Petersburg, a beautiful city that does not exist any more after the Revolution in 1917, Petersburg was renamed Petrograd, and then Leningrad. Following the collapse of Communism in Russia, it has reverted to its original name but when the novel was published Petersburg was still called Leningrad

sphinx a mythical creature, half human, half lion, renowned in Greek mythology for its riddle

hieratic priestly, priestlike, associated with sacred mysteries

At the command of the Prince, the rocks of the wilderness transformed ... St Petersburg was built out of a marshy wilderness on the orders of Tsar Peter the Great (1672–1725), after whom it was named

hyperbole exaggeration

wagon lit sleeping carriage in a train (French)

Sybil in Greek mythology the sibyls could see into the future, but their prophecies were always very difficult to interpret

John the Baptist's [head] on a platter in Matthew 14:1–12, the story of John the Baptist's execution is told. John offended Herod's wife, Herodias, and she plotted against him. Her daughter danced for Herod, and he promised her whatever she wanted. She asked for John's head to be presented to her on a silver charger (or tray). The image of John's head was a very popular one at the turn of the century, but it is here reduced to the level of farce in its relation with a pig wearing a ruff

Ludic Game Kearney's tautologous description of the life of the circus: literally, the playful game

Monsieur Lamarck's Educated Apes ironically, given Lamarck's degenerate character in the novel, the name Lamarck is also that of a famous French naturalist, Jean-Baptiste de Monet Lamarck (1744–1829). The original Lamarck argued, prefiguring elements of Darwin's theories, that the

characteristics of a species evolved from generation to generation. The
Lamarck in the novel shows that evolution can go backwards

empyrean highest heaven

caballero cavalier, knight (Spanish)

neophytes converts, beginners or novices

cimex lectularius bedbug (Latin)

Hannibal's tuskers the Carthaginian general, Hannibal, marched across the
Alps against the Roman empire, with elephants as pack animals and cavalry
in *c.*218BC

CHAPTER 2   Walser acquaints himself with the circus apes while
the Ape-Man's woman and the Strong Man make love
in a corner of the ring. A tiger breaks into the ring.
The Strong Man and the apes escape. Walser and the
Ape-Man's woman are left to face the tiger

The circus building in Petersburg is a permanent building, not a tent.
The narrative takes us through the public entrance, past the glittering
champagne bar, up the stairs to the red-plush seats and boxes around the
arena. Walser, however, enters the circus by the back door.

The ring is occupied by Lamarck's Educated Apes, watched over
by the Ape-Man's woman. The apes appear to be rehearsing their
schoolchildren's routine, but when Walser creeps closer he realises
that they are perhaps participating in a real school lesson. Before he can
verify his impression, however, he trips over his long clown's shoes and
makes a noise that disturbs the apes. The chief chimp, the Professor,
exchanges a knowing look with Walser who realises that the apes are
more 'human' than they appear. The Professor leads Walser into the
ring. He asks him to remove his clothes, and commences a comparative
anatomy lesson. Elsewhere in the ring, the Strong Man and the
Ape-Man's woman are energetically engaged in sexual intercourse. The
chimps examine Walser's body in detail, but are most interested in
his speech. He has just begun a speech from *Hamlet*, as the Strong
Man and the Ape-Man's woman achieve their climax, when the shout
goes up that a tiger has escaped, and Sybil the pig races through the ring,
hotly pursued by a large striped cat. The apes escape, as does the Strong
Man. Walser might have got away too, but he turns and sees the

Ape-Man's woman, encumbered by her underwear, and he sets out to tackle the tiger.

This chapter asks the reader to confront one of the most significant questions raised by the novel as a whole: what is the nature of our own humanity? The setting of the Imperial State Circus is one in which animality and spirituality are seen to coexist. The luxurious setting of plush and gilt is belied by the 'aroma of horse dung and lion piss' (p. 105). It exhibits the 'rather queasy luxury that always seemed to have grime under its fingernails', so that once again, appearance and reality are at odds with each other. There is an insistence on the materiality of bodies that have to function as bodies; the emphasis is on the fact that both people and animals exhibit the same bodily needs for food, sex and defecation. The lovely ladies who visit the circus wearing fur and French perfume are much more closely related to the animals in the circus from whom the furs and the perfumes are derived than they would like to believe.

This is the setting for Walser's uncomfortable realisation that animals and people are not so different – not nearly as different as *people* would like to believe. When he looks into the face of the Professor, he sees his own humanity reflected back at him:

Walser never forgot this first, intimate exchange with one of these beings whose life ran parallel to his, this inhabitant of the magic circle of difference, unreachable … but not unknowable; this exchange with the speaking eyes of the dumb. It was like the clearing of a haze. Then the Professor, as if acknowledging their meeting across the gulf of strangeness, pressed his tough forefinger down on Walser's painted smile, bidding him be silent. (p. 108)

Speech is what appears to separate animals from people, as will be seen later in relation to the Princess of Abyssinia's tigers (see Petersburg, Chapter 5). In the case of the chimpanzees, speech appears to be the *only* point of separation, for when Walser entered the ring, what he came across was not a rehearsal for the apes' performance, but a *real* school lesson. Performance has become reality in the topsy-turvy world of the circus, where all the usual rules are broken. This is made more evident by the ironic juxtaposition of the apes' intellectual pursuits with the sexual congress of the Ape-Man's woman and the Strong Man. While the animals' behaviour is human, the people, as it were, behave like animals.

One of the questions that the chapter asks, therefore, is what is it about human beings that makes them feel that they are so much superior to the beasts? Walser is required by the apes to strip and to show them his body in intimate detail: the anatomy lesson of which he is the central exhibit takes place in the context of the Strong Man and the Ape-Man's woman also stripping for action for an anatomy lesson of their own. Walser ends up comically naked except for the dunce's cap put on his head by one of the apes, and his clown's make-up, a figure of fun rather than one exhibiting human nobility. In this circumstance it is clear that his own body is not so different from the bodies of the apes. The key interest for the apes, though, is Walser's ability to speak. The Professor examines his mouth, and, as the 'grunts of the Strong Man began to accelerate' (p. 110), Walser begins to recite Shakespeare's lines about the amazing attributes of humanity. The bathos of juxtaposing the sex scene in the background with the anatomy lesson and poetic language of the foreground points to the possibility that 'a man' is not necessarily a wonderful piece of work.

What happens next shows that Walser is human in a way that the apes and even the Strong Man are not. When the tiger erupts into the ring the apes and the Strong Man run away, leaving the Ape-Man's woman for tiger meat (she cannot run because her knickers are round her ankles – a comically incongruous detail in this dangerous situation). Walser thinks about running away; but when the woman screams he turns back and sets out to confront the tiger. His own self-image of what it means to be a man prevents him from sacrificing another human being to his own safety. In the end, speech accompanied by altruism might define humanity. At the close of the chapter, though, the reader is left dangling, not knowing whether Walser's manliness is about to end up inside a tiger: there is a deferral, a putting off, of our knowledge to the next chapter, like a cliffhanger in an old-fashioned serial. Because of the

comic context of the novel as a whole, though, we can easily guess
that all will be well.

caryatids pillars carved in the shape of female figures
Bechstein renowned as the best brand of piano
Gaugin Paul Gaugin (1848–1903), French painter who settled in Tahiti,
famous in particular for his depictions of native women
uroboric snake the uroborus is the snake that eats its own tail; it is hence
often used as an image for a never-ending circle, that is, as a metaphor
for infinity
Balinese dancers a topical reference in the 1890s, when dancers from the
Far East had enjoyed an enormous vogue in the music halls and nightclubs
of Western Europe
'What a piece of work is man! How noble in reason! How infinite in faculty!'
from *Hamlet*, II.2.303–4. In the circumstances, the quotation is ironic
Lot's wife-like proverbially, Lot's wife was turned into a pillar of salt for
looking back on the city of Sodom which God was about to destroy. See
Genesis 19:26

CHAPTER 3   Walser meets Fevvers again, as she tends his wounds

When Walser comes round he is in Fevvers's dressing room. She is
tending his wounds without much gentleness. She explains that when he
charged the tiger (or, rather tigress), the cat took a swipe at him, but was
in turn knocked off her feet by a blast of icy water from the Princess of
Abyssinia's hosepipe. Fevvers seems cross, in part because the journalist
is in Petersburg at all, in part because she believes that his nakedness was
because it was he who was having sex with the Ape-Man's woman.
Patched and bandaged, Walser is sent back to Clown Alley. From the
monkey house comes the sound of the Ape-Man beating his woman.

There are a number of short chapters in this novel, punctuating
longer stretches of narrative with very swift resolution of action, and
this is one such. Its primary function is to relieve the suspense of the
ending of Chapter 2. Walser, we quickly realise, is not dead.
Though the tiger did attack him, he was only wounded in the
shoulder before the Princess of Abyssinia blasted the cat with
ice-cold water. Walser has a wounded arm; he also has severely
wounded pride: he goes home 'painfully aware that, by the very

"heroicness" of his extravagant gesture, he had "made a fool of himself"' (p. 114). The all-action hero has been made to look silly, an example of the mock heroic in action.

The second function of the chapter is to undo Walser's incognito. Until now, Fevvers had not known that the journalist was at the circus. His clown's make-up is an effective disguise. Now she does know, and she is not pleased, though it is difficult to say whether her irritation is because he is there at all, or because she believes that it was Walser, not the Strong Man, who was 'having it off with the Ape-Man's missus' (p. 114). Whatever the case, the injured Walser 'felt himself much diminished' in Fevvers's eyes, and he does not like this feeling. We should be wondering why he cares so much.

CHAPTER 4   On his return to Clown Alley, Walser is treated to the philosophy of the clowns, and to a display of their talents

When Walser gets back to Clown Alley, the clowns are gathered for their evening meal, presided over by Buffo the Great, the clown chief. Buffo's mode of clowning is 'violent slapstick' (p. 117). In his performances, things fall apart in his hands, he simulates killing other clowns, he dies and cannot be fitted into his coffin, he is resurrected and frightens the children in the audience. In his private life he is a melancholy drunkard. During the meal, he begins to describe the philosophy of clowning.

Clowns, he argues, are figures of despair. They are clowns because they have failed in some other area of life, and they are humiliated by the laughter they provoke. At the same time, clowns are also figures who have chosen the particular manner of their humiliation, like Christian martyrs. He tells the story told of every great clown. When suffering the very depths of despair he performed at his absolute best. In a bar later that night, out of his clown disguise, he was depressed and sad. The bartender told him to go and see the Great Buffo who would cheer him up. No one, he suggests, can ever make a clown laugh. The only claim that a clown can make is that he has made himself. His costume and make-up are his own character written on his face. The price of this is that there is no one behind the clothes and the wig and the mask of wet white. A clown without his clown's face is no one at all.

Now the twin clowns, Grik and Grok, begin to hum, and the clowns all begin to dance. Their dance is anarchic. They throw food, crockery and vodka bottles at each other. They perform obscene gestures with false phalluses, balloon testicles, and bottles pushed up bottoms. From the soup cauldron, Buffo produces obscene objects such as lavatory brushes, chamber pots and lavatory paper. Walser still feels sore from his encounter with the tiger. He steps outside for a breath of air, and is accosted by a tiny figure who throws herself at his feet, weeping and kissing him.

Fevvers tells Walser later in the novel that she cannot stand clowns (p. 143). For her, there is something inhuman and uncanny about them. This chapter, which deals with clown philosophy in detail, suggests why they give her the creeps. Theirs is a topsy-turvy world in which normality exists only in an exaggerated form (the large features painted on their faces), and where obscenity and anarchy lurk very near the surface. Buffo, as the narrative comments, is a huge man, over seven feet tall, whose trademark is physical clumsiness and violent slapstick. Violence is apparent even in his appearance, which is an assault on conventional decency:

Buffo the Great, the terrible Buffo, hilarious, appalling, devastating Buffo with his round, white face and the inch-wide rings of rouge round his eyes, and his four-cornered mouth, like a bow tie, and, mockery of mockeries, under his roguishly cocked, white, conical cap, he wears a wig that does not simulate hair. It is, in fact, a bladder. Think of that. He wears his insides on his outside, and a portion of his most obscene and intimate insides, at that; so that you might think he is bald, he stores his brains in the organ which, conventionally, stores piss. (p. 116)

Everything about the clowns is exaggerated and to some degree disgusting. Buffo performs extravagant pratfalls over the smallest objects. He makes his body behave as though he is not really in control of it. He 'is himself the centre that does not hold' (p. 117), a figure of anarchy and danger. The clowns perform to make their audience laugh, but it is uneasy laughter since it is dependent on humiliation (of the clowns) and cruelty (in the audience). The audience laughs at a martyrdom, in Buffo's own analogy; it is entertainment made out of horror, hence his blasphemous sense of himself as Christ, and of the martyrdoms of saints as 'the acts in a great circus' (p. 120).

While the novel as a whole consistently argues for a version of human life in which conventions are not accepted at face value, it implies that the clowns take this tendency too far. Their act performs violence in the form of slapstick. But violence, Angela Carter seems to suggest, is never funny. At the end of the previous chapter, Walser has returned to Clown Alley from Fevvers's hotel to the sound of the Ape-Man beating his woman 'as though she were a carpet' (p. 115). There is no sense in which the real beating is supposed to be seen as funny: why, then, is the performance of violence supposed to provoke laughter? To laugh at the clowns is to demonstrate one's own loss of innocence. As Buffo has said: 'The child's laughter is pure until he first laughs at a clown' (p. 119).

'The beauty of clowning is,' says Buffo, 'nothing ever changes' (p. 117). But this is also its danger. The novel's whole ethos is about development – about changing things that are wrong, learning from experience. The fact that clowning never changes makes it impossible for clowning to develop, to evolve into something more humane than laughter at Christians thrown to the lions (or tigers in this case). The claim of autonomy – that is, the claim that clowns have made themselves (p. 121) – is scarcely a proud boast in this context. 'What a piece of work is man', Walser mused before the tiger got him: if the clown makes himself, the narrative implies, he definitely ought to be a better self-creation than a man who wears a bladder on his head, who regresses to a childish obsession with anality, and who dances to celebrate 'the primal slime' (p. 125). The chimps, Walser theorised, were 'grappling with Darwin's theory – from the other end' (p. 110). The chimps were trying to rise above their condition; the clowns are emblems of a degeneration that is, in Fevvers's words, 'a crime against humanity' (p. 143).

in the place where Leonardo seats the Christ Leonardo da Vinci's fresco, *The Last Supper* (*c*.1497), depicts Christ at the centre of a long table, with six disciples seated on either side of him

Things fall apart ... He is himself the centre that does not hold an allusion to W.B. Yeats's poem 'The Second Coming' (1919)

acolytes attendants or assistants, novices

Pierrot the clown character from traditional French pantomime. The Pierrot is a sad clown, a melancholy figure, with ghastly white face and exaggerated black eyes and mouth

Catherine … St Lawrence … Saint Sebastian … St Jerome St Catherine of Alexandria (d. AD307) was supposed to be martyred on a wheel set with razors, but the wheel broke and she was beheaded instead; St Lawrence (d. AD258) was roasted to death on a gridiron; St Sebastian (d. AD288) was tied to a tree or pillar and shot with arrows; St Jerome (c.AD342–420) was a hermit and ascetic who communed with a lion in his cell

Domenico Biancolette … Grimaldi … Jean-Gaspard Deburau all famous clowns from earlier centuries

a thing that, had he not been invented, should have been an allusion to French philosopher Voltaire (1694–1778): 'If God did not exist, it would be necessary to invent him.'

Darby and Joan these names, originally derived from a poem written in the eighteenth century, have become proverbial for a loving, old married couple

'*Nothing* will come of nothing' from Shakespeare's *King Lear*, I.1.92

bergomask a rustic dance associated with the district of Bergamo in Italy

her too, too solid kitchen an allusion to *Hamlet*, II.1.129: 'O! that this too, too solid flesh would melt …'

Madonna of Misericordia one of the guises of the Virgin Mary, Our Lady of Sorrows or Pity

CHAPTER 5   Mignon's life story

The tiny figure at Walser's feet is the Ape-Man's woman, whose name is Mignon. She is pathetically bruised and tear-stained, and Walser does not know what to do with her. He takes her to Fevvers to seek advice. When they get to her suite, Fevvers seems to be in a very bad mood. When she sees Mignon, though, her good nature reasserts itself; while Mignon goes to have her bruised body bathed by Lizzie, we are told her life story.

Mignon was the daughter of a man who killed his wife and subsequently drowned himself. She became a street child in the city where she lived by petty thieving, selling flowers and casual prostitution. (Meanwhile, Mignon is enjoying her bath and she begins to sing. Her voice is arresting.) Her life on the streets was very hard. She was rescued by Herr M., a medium, who took her in to work for him. Herr M. operated a scam for which he needed an assistant. Her job was to 'pose for the dead' (p. 128). Herr M. would persuade the grieving relatives of dead girls that he could contact the dead. Because 'All young girls look the same after a long illness' (p. 135), he used Mignon, dressed in a nightgown, with her hair loose, as a stand-in for the dead girl. She would 'appear' to the relatives, and he would photograph her, charging a large fee for a picture from the spirit world. When Herr M. was exposed as a fraud and sent to prison, Mignon's livelihood disappeared and she was thrown back on her own resources. She began to work as a waitress and singer in a bar. One night, a gentleman with a chimp began to court her through the good offices of the ape, known as the Professor. She ran away to the circus with him, but the Ape-Man abused her. He beat her every night. She was also the sexual prey of any male circus figure who chose to take her.

With Mignon's story brought to the present, and her bath almost over, Fevvers has tears running down her face as she listens to Mignon sing. Walser, too, is strangely moved, either because of Mignon's song, or because of Fevvers's tears. When Mignon emerges from the bathroom, Fevvers feeds her, before arranging something that Walser does not understand with a Russian waiter. She sends Mignon and Walser off to the bridal suite to consummate their relationship. But Walser cannot bear the idea, and rushes from the room.

> This chapter is structured by two different time frames. This is, of course, the structure of the novel as a whole. Fevvers's story is set in 1899–1900, but the narrative was constructed in 1983–4, so that there is a whole order of historical knowledge available to narrator and readers which is hidden from the characters. In this chapter, there is the present of the narrative, where Fevvers is clearly jealous and is angry with Walser, and where she is kind to Mignon, feeding her and bathing her; but there is also the narrative of Mignon's life story, told as a series of flashbacks from the present of the narrative (the technical term is analepsis) to give us the details of Mignon's life to date.
>
> Mignon's story is the case history of the abused child: the daughter of a murderer and a whore; a street child who turned to crime

and prostitution; a young woman exploited and abused. (Angela
Carter may well have been thinking of the case studies of Sigmund
Freud and mocking their authority in the narrative of Mignon's
history. The medium's name, Herr M., is exactly the kind of
designation that Freud gave to patients and their families in
his case histories.) Mignon is the classic victim, completely passive
in the face of her experiences. She brings together two of Angela
Carter's most important political themes. Mignon is exploited
because of poverty, a victim of unfair economic systems; and
she is exploited because of her gender, the victim of the inequality
of women. But she is also exploited because of her own
character. Because she is so passive, she is easy meat. She was very
nearly literally easy meat to the tigress, prevented from running
because encumbered by her underwear, only able to scream. She
lacks the articulacy to analyse her situation (through the novel she
scarcely speaks at all); and she lacks the strength of will to do
anything about it – for Mignon, being beaten is 'an expectation
that is always fulfilled' (p. 141). She is a walking opportunity for
brutal men.

His attempt to rescue her again gives Walser an opportunity to
demonstrate his own humanness. He is a different kind of man
from most of those that Mignon has met before. Not only did
he, at some personal cost, try to rescue her from the tiger when
the Strong Man ran away; at the end of this chapter, he also refuses
to exploit her – though it may be that he does the right thing
because his arm still hurts from the tiger attack. We also see Walser
learning the pain of emotion in this chapter. When Fevvers weeps
at Mignon's song he feels pain in his heart, because he too is moved
by the song, and because he is moved by Fevvers's emotion. This is
an improvement on the young objective journalist who arrived to
interview Fevvers at the beginning of the novel with no capacity to
feel at all. Walser's character is developing.

Mignon Mignon's name literally means 'beloved, darling, favourite' (French).
She is also associated with the character Mignon from the German novel
Wilhelm Meister's Apprenticeship by Johann Wolfgang von Goethe
(1749–1832). In the novel, Mignon is the daughter of an incestuous union

of two circus performers. The hero rescues her from her circus life, but never notices that she is pining for him. She dies of her love

So we'll go no more a-roving … And the moon shine still as bright poem by George Gordon, Lord Byron (1788–1824)

fauteuils armchairs (French)

Praxinoscope, Phasmatrope, Zoopraxiscope types of early camera

CHAPTER 6   A summary of Walser's feelings

Walser is confused. He is confused because he had come to Petersburg to be a *journalist dressed as a clown*; but because he cannot write with his wounded arm, he appears to have become a *real* clown. He is also confused because he has fallen in love with Fevvers, but she has treated him with varying degrees of contempt since they have known each other, and he does not know what to do.

This chapter, less than a page long, is a kind of punctuation mark. Walser's character is changing with the progress of the novel. He is consequently feeling disoriented. The narrative offers two reasons for this confused state. The first has to do with his professional life. For men at the end of the nineteenth century – and, indeed, into the twentieth century – professional life was an indication of identity: the working man *was* what he did. Walser came to Petersburg as a journalist wearing clown clothes and make-up as a disguise. Since he has hurt his arm however, he cannot write, so that the disguise has become the reality: the illusion has become the authentic self. At the same time, he has fallen in love. It is usual that love is described in literature as an unsettling emotion. But perhaps particularly for Walser, the stirring of his emotions is something he is unprepared for: he used to be a war correspondent, paid to be impassive in the face of awesome events. Now he has nothing to hide behind. In *Hamlet*, a play with which Walser is clearly acquainted, Hamlet is often regarded as becoming mad because he has acted the part of madness: the boundary between performance and the authentic self has dissolved. This may be what is happening to Walser. He is losing his sense of himself as a stable identity – the process that began with time being out of joint that night in London continues apace.

CHAPTER 7   Morning rehearsals at the circus. Walser learns to be a
Human Chicken. Fevvers and Lizzie secure Mignon's
future, and find a way to send letters home without the
interference of the secret police

A freezing morning in the courtyard at the circus. The trapeze artist
children, the Charivaris, practise high-wire walking. Hawkers and
vendors sell their wares. Colonel Kearney wanders amongst his circus
performers purring with satisfaction. The tigers are restive, waiting for
their morning rations. Their keeper, the Princess of Abyssinia, never
speaks and so retains an air of mystery. Her act consists of her playing the
piano in demure evening dress for a dance of the tigers. The tigers enter
first; then she comes in and sits down with her back to them – the only
time when she is afraid of them. In case of accidents she always has a
loaded gun on top of the piano. She does not speak because she has
learned that the tigers do not like it. Her body is covered with claw marks
as testimony to their power.

Next Samson, the Strong Man, comes into the ring to shouts of
derision because his girlfriend has run off with a clown. He is furious,
threatening to beat Walser up when he gets the chance. Then Fevvers
enters with Lizzie. Lizzie throws money to a gypsy fiddler, and accepts a
piece of paper – perhaps a ballad – from him. The peddler of hot jam pies
is really a secret policeman, and would have been interested in the
transaction, but Fevvers has distracted him by buying up all his stock for
the Charivari children. Fevvers and Lizzie have Mignon with them,
though no one recognises her now she is clean and properly dressed.
Fevvers leads the way to the Princess's tiger enclosure.

The next arrivals are the clowns. The star attraction of this rehearsal
is Walser who is about to learn his routine. He crows like a Russian cock,
'Cock-a-doodle-dooski' (p. 152), and flaps his arms like wings: he has
become the Human Chicken. The other clowns begin to pelt him with
so many eggs that he is blinded; he lashes out at them, but cannot catch
them, and his gestures of real frustrated fury are the funniest part of his
act. The Human Chicken will, from now on, be a major part of the
Clowns' Christmas dinner routine.

Near the tiger enclosure, Fevvers is negotiating with the Princess
about Mignon. She suggests that Mignon might sing to the tigers while

the Princess plays. At first, the Princess is unwilling, and Mignon is terrified. But Fevvers is persuasive. Mignon is pushed into the cage with the Princess, and she begins to sing. The tigers are mesmerised, and the Princess suddenly realises that she need no longer be afraid for that moment before she begins to play: Mignon joins her act.

The circus courtyard begins to empty: the Charivari children have had to go to bed because they have stomach-ache from eating jam pies. Fevvers and Lizzie are delighted with their morning's work. As they cross the courtyard to return to their hotel, they spot Walser, washing off egg debris from his face. Fevvers is in a much better mood now she knows that he did not sleep with Mignon. She flirts with him. Then Lizzie demands to know how Walser is able to get his despatches past the secret police censor. The answer is that he sends them in diplomatic bags via the British Embassy. With his wounded arm, he cannot write: which leaves all the more room for Lizzie and Fevvers's '*letters home*' (p. 156). Lizzie produces a bundle of letters from her handbag to be despatched in just that way.

This chapter is a set piece, like the crowd scenes that are sometimes part of movies. It does not appear to move the plot very far forward. Yet several small details released here will be significant later on. The narrative performs the kind of sleight of hand that it also describes in its content. When Fevvers and Lizzie enter the circus they distract attention away from the gypsy fiddler handing Lizzie a piece of paper by mobbing the seller of jam pies. Attention is focused away from where the real action is taking place. The reader who pays careful attention to the scene might also have wanted to know what the exchange of paper and money was all about. But Fevvers's extravagance distracts the pieman; and the narrative's refusal to dwell on this detail distracts the reader's curiosity – we are moved on to the next thing without time to notice what is going on. The narrative behaves like a conjuring trick: now you see it, now you don't. But if you don't pay attention, you'll end up being bamboozled, to quote the Colonel. The jam pies are important for another reason. They don't just stop us from noticing that Lizzie is a dangerous anarchist; they also provide an additional reason for the Charivari family to resent the arrival of Fevvers on the scene. The children who eat the pies have to go to bed with tummy ache, for which 'Mama blamed Fevvers' (p. 156). This will soon have consequences for the star. Similarly, the Colonel's plot to plant false information in the newspapers (the news that Fevvers is to marry the Prince of Wales) will also send shock waves through the narrative at a later point, though it seems unimportant now. When Walser began to listen to Fevvers's life story in London in part one, he started to lose his ability to unthread the narrative, to separate fact from fiction, significant from trivial detail. The proliferation of detail in this chapter plays that same trick on the reader.

The other two centres of the crowd scene are Walser's training as a Human Chicken, and the hiring of Mignon as the Princess's assistant. The first of these events reiterates the unease the narrative evokes about the nature of clowning. Again, it is emphasised that the laughter provoked by the clowns depends on rage and humiliation: Walser gets into a frenzy about being pelted with eggs, but is told afterwards 'that his baulked gestures of fury were the funniest thing' (p. 153); *real* anger, *real* humiliation, and the *real* pain of his wounded arm make an uncomfortable kind of comedy.

The introduction of Mignon to the Princess and the tigers is significant in a different way. It picks up on the theme of the 'humanity' of animals explored earlier with the Educated Apes. The tigers are less intelligent than the chimps, but physically much more powerful. Their frustrations about their inability to speak always risk, therefore, turning into violence. This is why the Princess does not speak to them. Her music has charms to soothe the savage beast but speech does not. Articulate, functional language is an insult to beautiful animals who cannot speak it. Mignon's song is perfect for this context. Not only is it soothingly musical; it is also strangely inarticulate, since Mignon is singing words that she does not understand, 'even though they were in her own language' (p. 154). If the Princess chooses to be speechless, Mignon also has an attenuated relationship with language – words do not express her consciousness, indeed, she almost has no consciousness. Mignon will learn the uses of language as the text progresses; Walser, on the other hand, the articulate figure of the journalist, will eventually be robbed of both speech and consciousness, and will have to learn to speak and think and be all over again.

Breughel Pieter Breughel (*c*.1520–69), Dutch painter famous for lively scenes of peasant life

deshabille usually spelled *déshabillé*; the state of partial undress (French)

kvass Russian rye beer

Argyrol brand name of a patent disinfectant

'Quelle chantooze! ... Quelle spectacle!' Fevvers's French is spoken with a bad accent. The word should be *chanteuse*: 'what a singer, what a spectacle!'

Kali the Hindu goddess of destruction

'Elle s'appelle Mignon. C'est vachement chouette, ça' 'She's called Mignon. She's really sweet.' (French)

nature morte literally 'dead nature' (French), meaning 'still life'

the song that was written for [Mignon] before she was born ... Do you know the land where the lemon trees grow? 'Kennst du das land' ('Do you know the land') is the song that Mignon sings in *Wilhelm Meister's Apprenticeship* (see note on Chapter 5)

CHAPTER 8   Fevvers's trapeze is sabotaged. The Charivaris are sacked. Mignon and Walser start a new act. The Strong Man takes his revenge on Walser; Walser is rescued by Fevvers. The Professor 'sacks' the Ape-Man from the Educated Apes act and renegotiates the apes' contract with Kearney

Fevvers is rehearsing in the ring. The Charivaris are not very pleased with her arrival on the scene. They have an illustrious history and they don't like this upstart. They gather to watch her. Walser too has come to watch. As Fevvers reaches out for a trapeze and launches her weight on to it, there is a snapping sound and the rope breaks. She slowly swings herself to catch the second trapeze on the other side of the Big Top. Then she sits on it and stays there.

All hell has broken loose below. Lizzie, convinced that the rope has been severed by the Charivaris, starts swearing at them, and they swear back. The broken rope has indeed been cut and everyone believes that the

Charivaris have done it. The Colonel knows that he will have to fire them or lose Fevvers.

Fevvers comes down once the Charivaris have been sacked. Walser cannot tell whether she is shaken or not as they all settle to watch Mignon audition for the Colonel. Mignon sings her song, and though the Colonel is impressed, he wonders if the act might not be a little too high class for the circus: Sybil the pig is also dubious. He asks what else she can do, and she begins to waltz with a tiger to the Princess's accompaniment. It brings the house down. Next a volunteer is required to dance with tiger's mate. The tigress is jealous of Mignon's dance with her mate and an unwilling Walser is pushed into the ring – she is the same tigress who had tried to eat him. Mignon and the tiger and Walser and the tigress waltz in the ring to great applause.

Despite this triumph Walser still gets beaten up by the Strong Man. With his wounded arm he cannot defend himself, and it takes Fevvers with a hosepipe to separate the two of them. The two wet, bruised men are taken by Fevvers to the Princess's lodgings where the Strong Man tearfully declares his love for Mignon. While they are all sitting around the cat-house, the Professor enters the scene, dragging the drunken Ape-Man behind him. The Strong Man is despatched to put the drunk in his bunk, and Fevvers suggests that the rest of the company leave the Princess and Mignon alone to enjoy some privacy. When the Strong Man returns, they are singing new songs together, and he is shut out, which makes him weep all over again.

Meanwhile, in the Ape-Man's lodgings, the Professor is emptying Lamarck's pockets, searching for the circus contract. He finds it, tears it up, and goes off to find the Colonel. The Professor is insistent that he must have a new contract from the Colonel; the chimps must be paid more, and directly to the Professor, and Lamarck should be sacked. The Colonel consults Sybil and she declares that the new contract is 'Cheap at the price' (p. 169). A new contract is drawn up and the Professor leaves.

> When the clowns performed their dance in Clown Alley it was a
> dance of disintegration and chaos. That dance prefigures what is
> now starting to happen to the circus. Instead of being a tight-knit
> community of workers all aiming at the same goal of entertaining

the audience, the circus is riven with internal rivalries and disagreements. The Charivari troupe's sabotage of Fevvers's trapeze at the beginning of the chapter is the first example of the breakdown of what is supposed to be backstage camaraderie. Sawing through the trapeze rope dismantles the very fabric of the circus, and threatens its existence. The Professor's dissatisfaction with his employer, Lamarck, and his renegotiation of the apes' contract with the Colonel, is the second. The apes are clearly planning their own escape.

At the same time, while some parts of the circus are in turmoil, other parts of the performance are being honed. Mignon and Walser's tiger dance is a complete success, and will bring the house down. But it is a dangerous success because, like the ape act, it dissolves the boundaries between human and beast. As Walser revolves around the enclosure he has another moment of revelation, like the one he had earlier with the Professor (see p. 108):

> Mignon whirled by, flashed the clown a brilliant smile and Walser, supported by the unforged steel of the tigress's forepaws, thought: There goes Beauty and the Beast. Then, looking into the tigress's depthless, jewelled eyes, he saw reflected there the entire alien essence of a world of fur, sinew and grace in which he was the clumsy interloper and, as the tigress steered his bedazzlement once more round the Princess's white piano, he allowed himself to think as the tigers would have done:
>
> Here comes the Beast, and Beauty! (p. 164)

The moment of revelation does not last because the tigress has very bad breath from the diet of raw meat that she eats. As so often in the novel, a significant insight is partially debunked by its juxtaposition with an unpleasant material fact that distracts the thinker from his thought. Moreover, this is the very tigress with whom Walser had had such a narrow escape after the apes' anatomy lesson: he is only too aware of the beastliness that resides in her beauty. But for that moment, he is unsettled in his own humanity – he is the beast to the tigress's beauty.

The bestiality of man is once again demonstrated by the figure of Samson, the Strong Man, a man who lives his life in a leopard-skin loincloth – wearing the skin of a beast, and depending on brute strength for his livelihood, like an animal. Indeed, when Walser is beaten up by Samson, Fevvers metes out to him exactly the same treatment as the Princess used on the rogue tigress: she blasts him with cold water. But the important thing about Samson is that he, like Walser, is capable of change. At first appearance, he is the epitome of the stupid man of strength: all muscles and no brains or finer feelings. When he sees Mignon in her new incarnation as pretty girl, however, he starts to develop a very primitive kind of sensibility. Unlike a true caricature figure (for example, Colonel Kearney), he will develop during the novel and become something other than a mere muscle man. He will put aside his machismo and discover his feminine side – and that process begins here: out of his broken heart, 'sensibility might poke a moist, new-born head' (p. 167). The metaphor is, of course, the metaphor of birth, and there is no more feminine, less macho, image than that.

gutta-percha a tough form of rubber

Nero, Charlemagne, the Borgias, Napoleon Nero was Roman emperor from AD54–68, and was renowned for cruelty and sensuous excess. Charlemagne was King of the Franks and Emperor of Western Europe between 768 and 814; he is particularly remembered for military prowess and for learning and culture, and is associated with the ideals of chivalry. The Borgias were a family of popes, princes and poisoners in the Italian Renaissance (active mostly in the sixteenth century). Their reputation rests on the strange combination of culture (they were responsible for commissioning some of the most famous works of art and buildings of the Renaissance) and violence – there were many murders of rivals ascribed to them. They were also supposedly sexually voracious. Napoleon Bonaparte (1769–1821) became Emperor of France after the French Revolution. He was a fearsome general, but was eventually defeated and exiled by the British and their European allies

lusus naturae game of nature, one of nature's tricks (Latin)

Lieder songs (German)

Onegin Eugene Onegin, a verse novel by Alexander Sergeevich Pushkin (1799–1837) was turned into an opera by Tchaikovsky in 1879

ensorcellating bewitching, enchanting

CHAPTER 9   **Fevvers and the Colonel have dinner, and the Colonel gets drunk. An unexpected gift of diamonds makes Fevvers's eyes light up**

Fevvers and the Colonel go out for a gargantuan meal. They eat and drink in vast quantities; but when they go to the Colonel's room for a nightcap, he falls into a drunken sleep, and Fevvers leaves. Back at the hotel Fevvers and Lizzie plan to send more '*letters home*' via Walser's diplomatic bag, and they discuss Walser's attractions. A bunch of flowers is delivered to the door. In their midst there is a diamond bracelet. We do not know who has sent it, but Fevvers is excited by the wealth it implies in her secret admirer.

> Another short chapter that again emphasises Fevvers's greed – for food, for money, and, if the circumstances are right, for sex. Colonel Kearney, despite his entrepreneurial skills, cannot perform because of drink. This does not bother Fevvers. On the other hand, the arrival of a diamond bracelet does excite her. She is a very material girl.
>
> **Britannia's revenge for the war of 1812** the War of 1812 between Britain and the United States was inconclusive. The Americans won the last battle of the war, but they did not achieve their goal of conquering Canada

CHAPTER 10   **The circus's last night is filled with disasters. Fevvers saves the show, before going off to an assignation with a Grand Duke. The apes desert the circus**

Fevvers is a triumph in St Petersburg. But she is weary of the process, and has agreed to only one supper date – with the mysterious admirer who has wooed her further with diamond earrings to match the bracelet he sent before. The date is set for the last night of the circus's stay in Petersburg.

Meanwhile, Buffo the Great has gone on a massive alcoholic spree to celebrate his last night in the city. Walser tries to warn the Colonel that his star clown is in no fit state to appear, but the Colonel keeps counting his takings.

At the beginning of that night's performance the circus parade of all the performers enters the ring. Buffo is roaring drunk. When the clowns appear Buffo has begun to hallucinate. He manages eventually to sit at the table set for the Clowns' Christmas dinner, while Walser, the Human Chicken, waits nervously in the wings, having been warned that Buffo, when drunk, can be homicidal. Lying on the table under a silver-plate dome, Walser bursts forth shouting 'Cock-a-doodle-doo', and Buffo tries to kill him with the carvers. He has gone completely mad. He chases Walser round and round the circus ring. Walser is saved by the Princess who blasts Buffo with a jet of icy water, and he is carried from the ring by Samson, the Strong Man. As Buffo is carried off to the madhouse, the show goes on with the tigers and the Princess and Mignon.

Walser goes to Fevvers's dressing room where the bird-woman and her dresser seem to be in the middle of a row. Fevvers flaunts her diamonds at Walser, when suddenly there is a terrible sound from the ring – the sound of a single shot. The tigress, Walser's dancing partner, has attacked Mignon out of jealousy, and the Princess has shot her. Fevvers is required immediately in the ring to save the show.

After her performance, Fevvers returns to the dressing room to prepare for her dinner with the aristocrat. Lizzie is worried that something will happen to her and warns her to be careful. Fevvers is irrepressible: she will be safe since she still carries her sword, and the meeting is worth it – she has been promised the diamond necklace that matches the bracelet if she turns up. She sets off in a glamorous carriage.

The circus is now being dismantled for the next stage of its journey. The Colonel is also losing some of his performers. The apes have had enough and depart for Helsinki. 'And, that night, [the Colonel] almost lost his star as well' (p. 183).

> The process of disintegration continues in this chapter. When Buffo the Great turns up so drunk he is hallucinating, the real meaning of the clowns' performances becomes clear. Instead of pretending to kill the Human Chicken, his aim is to do it for real. It is a brilliant performance, except for the fact that it is not a performance at all. All the jokes of the clowns' routine are made into literal fact by Buffo's incapacity. Illusion and reality collide with disastrous consequences. Hamlet pretends to be mad and goes mad; Walser pretends to be a clown and really becomes one; the clowns pretend to enact violence, and their act becomes violent. Living with the performance of anarchy disables Buffo's mind.

The second casualty is the tigress. She becomes jealous of Mignon dancing with her mate, and attacks the girl in Walser's absence. But what are tigers doing feeling jealousy anyway? The unnatural situation of the tiger act – the prim Princess in her white evening gown at her white piano, the tigers dancing – provokes unnatural feelings in them. The tigress cannot speak, so her emotion comes out as action. For a second time she nearly turns Mignon to meat. Just as disturbing, however, is the juxtaposition of Fevvers's departure for her assignation with the Grand Duke with the disposal of the tigress's body:

At the courtyard gate, a glamorous droshky stood ready receive her, behind the melancholy van from the knacker's yard. As a befurred footman handed Fevvers into the one, the Strong Man pitched the carcass into the other. (p. 182)

We are forewarned that Fevvers might also be about to become dead meat in the placing of those two details. We are also given a much more explicit message: 'And, that night, [the Colonel] almost lost his star as well' (p. 183). The 'almost' reassures the reader that the worst will not quite happen, but 'almost' also means that a bad event comes very close for a comic novel.

Yahoo in Jonathan Swift's *Gulliver's Travels* (1726) the Yahoos are the debased human inhabitants in a land ruled by gentle, intelligent horses named the Houyhnhnms
Jacob's with the angel Jacob wrestled with an angel for the blessing of God. See Genesis 32:24–32
tatterdemalion ragged, tattered, scarecrow-like
Kohinoor a very large diamond (over 100 carats in weight) whose name means Mountain of Light. It is now set in the British Crown Jewels
sham champagne
droshky carriage (Russian)

CHAPTER 11   **Fevvers goes to the Grand Duke's house and narrowly escapes disaster. She magically arrives, dishevelled and weeping, on the Trans-Siberian train**

The Grand Duke's house is a miracle of riches and luxury. Fevvers muses on the mystery of wealth and poverty as she marvels at the house, totting up the Duke's cash value as she goes. In his study, she discovers a full-size statue of herself made of ice, wearing the promised necklace. The Duke makes her nervous. He drinks a toast to her in vodka from 36 glasses that have been laid out to spell her real name, Sophia: but how does he know her name? She eats caviare before being entertained to a private viewing of the Duke's collection of automata: three almost life-size musicians. Although she knows that there are scientific explanations for all these wonders, the effect is uncanny. She is further unnerved when a drop of water splashes down from the melting ice statue.

The Duke then unveils his collection of jewelled eggs. He will give her whichever she chooses if she allows him to see her wings. Reluctantly, Fevvers agrees. When the eggs are opened up they contain miniaturised versions of chickens and eggs, and of a clockwork bird that sings Fevvers's own signature tune ('I'm only a bird in a gilded cage'). As she looks at the eggs, the Duke nuzzles her plumage, and she begins to masturbate him as part of the bargain for the necklace and the egg. When she unlooses her dress and the Duke begins to examine her body, he discovers Nelson's sword and snaps it in two on his knee. Now Fevvers is really frightened. But she continues to play the masturbatory game, and to coo over the eggs to buy more time. The next egg contains a miniature version of the Trans-Siberian railway train. As soon as she sees it Fevvers exclaims that this is the egg that she wants. The Duke, now reaching his climax under Fevvers's expert fingers, tries to dissuade her, wanting her to choose the next – which contains an empty gilded cage – but she holds on to the egg with the train. As the Duke achieves orgasm and the statue finally collapses, she pushes the train on to the carpet and runs after it. She is suddenly, inexplicably, on the Trans-Siberian train, being scolded and cared for by Lizzie and is in a very dishevelled and distressed state.

The second section ends, as had the first, with Fevvers in mortal danger from a powerful man. As with her encounter with Christian Rosencreutz, her meeting with the Grand Duke is motivated by material greed. In this case, diamonds are not a girl's best friend. The Grand Duke's residence is opulent, a palace of conspicuous consumption. The nature of his plans for Fevvers, though, is signalled by the life-size ice statue of her, wearing the diamond necklace she has been promised. The ice statue is of course doomed to melt. This is a portent of a serious threat to Fevvers – if her likeness is destroyed, what will become of her? As she wanders around the house, Fevvers, 'a girl of philosophical bent' (p. 185), makes clear her socialist/Marxist leanings. She ponders the nature of wealth, labour and productivity, and thinks of the exchange of sex for diamonds as an exercise in 'Property Redistribution' (p. 185).

She has not, however, bargained for the Grand Duke's power. Money can buy him anything he wants, from the automaton musicians to the fabulous Fabergé eggs, to Fevvers herself. Her value to him is her rarity value. He wants to possess and control her, which is as much of a threat to her autonomy and individuality as Rosencreutz's project of human sacrifice. 'May you melt in the warmth of my house just as *she* melts,' he says to Fevvers, referring to the ice statue (p. 186): it is a chilling wish. He knows her name, and Fevvers is disturbed by this as she was when Rosencreutz knew it – as if naming her with her proper name, Sophia, gives the namer power over her. The fantastic automata, themselves figures of the uncanny, who mimic life but are really machines, are a gruesome shock: Fevvers's common-sense attempt to explain them to herself ('there's a musical box inside the bird. And, anyone who could make a grandfather clock could put that harpy together.' p. 188) does not dismiss her fear.

One of the points that has been emphasised about Fevvers throughout the novel is that she is larger than life: 'she was a *big* girl' (p. 7), with heroic physical proportions and mental aptitude to match. The Grand Duke's jewelled eggs, on the other hand, are masterpieces of miniaturisation. Their effect depends not just on their material value (how expensive the jewels, the gold, the enamel effects are to produce), but on their resemblance to Chinese boxes, that image of infinity that Walser had originally applied to Fevvers's eyes, which had so disoriented him when he first met her (p. 30). These eggs contain worlds within worlds, each necessarily smaller than the last, so that eventually the image is diminished to nothingness:

For this one is made of pink enamel and opens up lengthwise to reveal an inner carapace of mother-of-pearl which, in turn, opens to reveal a spherical yolk of hollow gold. Inside the yolk, a golden hen. Inside the hen, a golden egg. Now we have diminished to the scale of Lilliput but we have not done yet; inside the egg there is the tiniest of picture-frames, set with minute brilliants. And what should the frame contain but a miniature of the *aerialiste* herself, in full spread as on the trapeze and yellow of hair, blue of eye as in life. (p. 189)

All around her, Fevvers is surrounded by the idea of herself shrinking. The statue gets smaller, her picture is miniature, and the egg that has been prepared to receive her contains a diminutive music box playing 'Only a bird in gilded cage', and an even more diminutive cage for her to step into. Size is part of Fevvers's power, but here it cannot help her. The Grand Duke is physically stronger than she is – he pins her down and breaks her sword. What Fevvers still has to save her, though, as she had had in her earlier near-fatal experience with Rosencreutz, is a will that refuses to submit to the expectation of her predators. Rosencreutz was furious that she had come armed, and that she answered him back. The Grand Duke expects her to submit to his vision of her as a bird in a gilded cage. Fevvers has other ideas. How she gets from the Duke's house to the train can only be explained as an instance of magic realism, when elements of the fantastic intrude on more or less ordinary experience. Psychologically though, the explanation is that Fevvers chooses the freedom of train travel over the fixed miniature space of the egg, and thereby makes good her escape.

capripede goat-footed
Croesus King Croesus is proverbial for his wealth
But neither does *this* one toil nor spin see Matthew 6:28
play at ducks and drakes to skim stones on the water
rara avis rare bird (Latin)
busts of Dante, Shakespeare, Pushkin Dante Alighieri (1265–1321), author of *The Divine Comedy*, William Shakespeare (1565–1616) and Alexander Pushkin (1799–1837), Russian poet and writer, are all regarded as exemplary figures in literature. The Grand Duke has representations of them in his library to suggest his own culture
versts Russian measure of length, equivalent to around two-thirds of a mile

trompe l'oeil literally, something that tricks the eye (French). An effect in painting by which the viewer is deceived into thinking that what s/he sees is real

Lilliput in *Gulliver's Travels*, Lilliput is the land of miniature people

PART THREE: SIBERIA

CHAPTER 1   The train journey through Siberia. The train is destroyed by an explosion. The human cargo is kidnapped by bandits

In the Trans-Siberian train, Fevvers is horrified by the boring journey and by the vastness of the landscape. Fevvers, unkempt, dark roots showing through her blond hair, cries for no apparent reason. In a different carriage the clowns play cards and try to forget Buffo's fate. Only the Colonel seems his usual happy self. He manages to pretend that everything is going well, despite the fact that the elephants are sickening in the cold. In the tigers' carriage, the Princess is uncomfortable around her cats: their trust has been broken by the shooting of the tigress. She plays organ music to keep them tranquil, and Mignon still sings, but something is not quite right.

In the dining car, the circus settles down to eat. As dessert is served, the train explodes into fragments. Fevvers is trapped under a table with a broken wing, but she manages to free herself. Lizzie, too, is safe, as is Mignon. The Princess is unconscious but appears to have no serious injuries. The Colonel and Sybil are also fine. Walser, however, has disappeared.

The tigers have turned into hot glass and disappeared into the mirrors from their carriage. The clowns all seem to have survived intact. The elephants, freed from their chains by the explosion, are trying to put out with their trunks the fire that the crash has started. And Fevvers is obsessively excavating the ruins of the dining car for some sign of Walser. These activities are interrupted by the arrival of a group of bandits, who kidnap the human survivors of the circus, and Sybil, at gunpoint.

For the first time since her narrative in Part One, this chapter is in part told in Fevvers's own voice – punctuated by the more usual third-person narrator. The distinction between the third-person narrator and Fevvers's narrative is difficult to unravel. Fevvers's voice is like the narrator's voice, and, at first, you would not necessarily know that it is she who is complaining about the endlessness of the tundra: 'I'm basically out of sympathy with landscape, I get the shivers on Hampstead bloody Heath' (p. 197). The differences between this narrative and Fevvers's description of her early life from the first part of the book have to do with her own position in the narrative. When she was telling her biography to Walser, she was *entertaining* the press. Her purpose was to play the part of the performer. Moreover, she knew what was coming next. From that position of power in the story, she has been reduced to someone speaking a story whose ending she does not know, and, away from an audience, her performance lacks sparkle. Her hair shows dark roots, she's not wearing make-up, and she's not properly dressed. The illusion of her perfection is disintegrating. Deprived of an audience, Fevvers has become introspective, and has even started to judge her own behaviour: 'Sometimes the lengths to which I'll go for money appal me', she comments to herself (p. 198). In the immediate context she is thinking about the journey – the geographical distance she will travel for money; but she is also thinking about her escape from the Grand Duke, another encounter linked with cash. Perhaps, like Walser, Fevvers is developing. The reasons for the change in her have to do with external circumstances: she is not performing at present; she is far away from where she can dye her hair or feathers. But they also have to do with her growing regard for Walser. She sees in him 'the vague, imaginary face of desire' (p. 204). The desire is compelling her to reassess some of her attitudes. Through this section of the novel, Fevvers's obsession with profit will diminish as her desire for Walser increases.

The train explosion is the real-life counterpart of the violent disintegration represented metaphorically by the clowns' dance. This is what will destroy the Colonel's ambition to emulate Hannibal. The elephants are doomed to die of pneumonia. Only human cargo is saved and then kidnapped from the train (not counting a few dogs from the clown troupe, and Sybil, who is a very human kind of pig). The chapter ends on a cliffhanger, as in Part Two, Chapter 2. Not only does Fevvers not know what is going to happen next to her, but Walser's fate is also again in doubt.

Cain Adam's son, cursed with a mark on his forehead for the murder of his brother, Abel, and exiled to the Land of Nod. See Genesis 4:1–18

cyclorama curved backdrop for a cinema or stage set, designed to give the illusion of perspective

lying on my belly like Miss O'Malley derivation obscure. Possibly a reference to Grace O'Malley, an Irish princess and pirate referred to by James Joyce in *Finnegans Wake* (1939); possibly a half-remembered playground rhyme

taiga marshy pine forest

Lucifers brand name of matches, named after the fallen angel Lucifer

gemütlich comfortable, cosy (German)

Limbo in Roman Catholic theology, Limbo is a borderland of hell, reserved for unbaptised children and ancestors born before Christ. It has come to mean any place of oblivion or nothingness

papirosse pink-papered cigarette (French)

Polyanna Pollyanna is the eponymous heroine of the 1913 novel by Eleanor H. Porter. Her key characteristic is her ability to be glad in every circumstance

macedonia a mixture of fruits served in syrup or jelly

Orpheus a mythical poet from ancient Thrace who could move even inanimate objects with the power of his music

CHAPTER 2   Walser is unconscious in the wreckage, where he will remain until he is dug out by a passing murderess

Walser remains buried in the wreckage. Indeed he gets more deeply buried because where he lies is where the elephants pile up the debris that they remove from the rest of the train. He might well have died there, but he will be rescued eventually by a murderess.

In the shortest chapter in the novel, we are reassured that Walser is not dead, and will not die, relieving Fevvers's fears, though, of course, Fevvers does not know it yet.

CHAPTER 3   There is a House of Correction filled with women
             prisoners near the train crash. The routines of the
             prison are described, as is the prison revolution

Not far from where the train has crashed stands a House of Correction.
It is run by Countess P., who poisoned her husband. It imprisons other
women who have also killed their husbands. The Countess's aim is to
make the murderesses repent. She forced them to build their prison, a
circular structure with a central tower from which she observes their every
move. When a prisoner repents she will be released: so far, no one has
ever left.

      One of the prisoners is Olga Alexandrovna, who took a hatchet
to a drunken husband when he beat her. The life of the prison is strictly
regulated, but there is nothing to pass the time. Instead, the prisoners
must contemplate their crimes under the gaze of the Countess in her
central tower. (She, like the wardresses who police the prison, is as much
a prisoner as the prisoners themselves.) The effect of this regime is
unexpected. Olga Alexandrovna contemplates her crime and decides that
she was justified. At the end of her third year inside she decides to do
something about her incarceration. The wardresses wear hoods so that
their faces cannot be seen. But they are vulnerable because their gloved
hands have to enter the cells to deliver food: so Olga Alexandrovna
reaches out to touch the woman who brings her food. Their eyes meet.
Contact has been made, and prisoner and wardress begin to correspond
with each other in letters hidden in food and toilet pails, written with
whatever materials come to hand. This one spark of love spreads like
wildfire through the prison, until everyone is touching and writing
letters. Finally an 'army of lovers' (p. 217) rises up against the Countess
and her regime. The cell doors are opened for the exercise hour, and the
prisoners never go back inside. The prisoners and the wardresses turn
on the Countess; they lock her inside her own tower and walk away from
the prison.

      At first sight, the prison seems oddly out of place in this narrative
      concerned with comic performances and fantasy, but the circus and
      the panopticon prison have quite a lot in common. Both, of course,
      are circular structures. What we have seen so far of circus life tends
      to suggest that the performers are imprisoned in their own world of

illusion, dependent for their existence on an applauding audience. There is no performance if there is no one to see it. Similarly, as far as the Countess P. is concerned, there is no discipline or repentance unless she sees it. But who is watching who? The round shape of the circus ring means that the audience is at least partly watching itself across the ring. Indeed, in Petersburg, where the circus is an opulent (if grimy) building, being seen there is probably as important as seeing the performance. If Countess P. is watching her charges from her central tower, they, in turn, are watching her: the prison makes prisoners of everyone. The circus turns even its audience into performers, breaking the boundary between stage and auditorium (indeed, the clowns habitually move amongst the audience).

This chapter also typifies Angela Carter's narrative strategy. It is based on a wide range of allusion: from Jeremy Bentham, to August Morel, to rum babas and menstrual blood. Linguists talk about the idea of register; that is, the appropriate language usage for a particular context. Angela Carter's narrative plays fast and loose with such notions of linguistic propriety. A prison cell described as if it were a cream cake is a somewhat unsettling and incongruously comic image (p. 211). Similarly, the blossoming of romantic love between prisoner and wardress does not at first sight seem very romantic:

Contact was effected, first, by illicit touch and glance, and then by illicit notes, or, if either guard or inmate turned out to be illiterate, by drawings made in and on all manner of substances, on rags of clothing if paper was not available, in blood, both menstrual and veinous, even in excrement, for none of the juices of the bodies that had been so long denied were alien to them, in their extremity (p. 217)

In its description of the clowns, the narrative had taken rather a dim view of the use of bodily functions for the purpose of violent comedy. Here, blood and excrement have turned, for want of anything better, to the uses of romance. The narrative approves of the ingenuity of love as it did not approve of the ingenuity of violence. It also sympathises with women who choose to love women. The relationship of the Princess and Mignon – a woman who has been constantly abused by men – is a love relationship;

here, in the prison, love is again exclusively female. When men have behaved so badly, why should women love them? And in this context, love is a powerful force, literally strong enough to break down prison walls. It is a utopian vision of the strength of love of women for women.

borsht and piroshkis beetroot soup and little meat or vegetable pies

a French criminologist who dabbled in phrenology probably a veiled allusion to Bénédict August Morel (1809–73), who studied the shapes of the heads of criminals (phrenology) to discover the physical types of criminality

panopticon from the Greek for 'all-seeing eye', a kind of prison building, built to a circular design, described by English philosopher Jeremy Bentham (1748–1832). The structure of the panopticon makes it impossible for prisoners to escape the gaze of the prison authorities

Tolstoy Leo Tolstoy (1828–1910), Russian novelist

baba au rhum rum baba (French), a kind of sponge cake

manned exclusively by women Angela Carter here highlights the contradictions of language: there is no feminine equivalent of the verb 'to man'

her courses were upon her a traditional way of saying that Olga was menstruating

CHAPTER 4   The prisoners find the wreckage of the train and Olga uncovers Walser

The women journey away from the prison towards the glow of the burning train. They find the elephants dead. They see the circus folk being led away by armed outlaws, whom they decide to avoid. They go to the train to see if they can help any remaining survivors, and to salvage what they can from the wreckage. They see the train as a 'treasure-trove of useful things' (p. 221) and begin to gather the things they will need for their new lives. They find the shattered mirror shards with the tigers' reflections on them and start to become anxious and superstitious about the train crash. All the women have to decide where they will go: back to Petersburg, to the lives they left behind, or forward into the unknown in Siberia. Olga is just thinking about whether she should return to the son she left behind when she hears a whimper in the background. It is Walser. Olga wakes him with a kiss and he calls her 'Mama'. He has lost his memory but is otherwise unhurt. She sets him on his feet and feeds him. Then the women hear the approach of the rescue train and make good their escape. They leave Walser to be rescued and disappear into the night. Walser, however, does not stay put. Shouting 'Cock-a-doodle-dooski!', he rushes into the forest in search of the women, but is stopped in his tracks by the sight of starlight in the snow.

Chapter 4 provides a fuller explanation of Walser's fate that is only hinted at in Chapter 2. The explosion has wiped him clean of all memory and all learned attributes. He is like a newborn child. It is this fact that makes Olga tender towards him. She has left her own child in Petersburg (he is, presumably, the same Little Ivan who lived in Clown Alley), and feels her maternal instinct tugging her when she sees Walser's helplessness. She kisses him awake and, just like a mother, feeds him and teaches him to walk again. Unlike a mother, however, she leaves him to his fate, assuming that the rescue train in the distance will pick him up. This does not happen because Walser is now so childlike, so capable of wonder, that he is excited by the image of starlight on snow, and moves away from the train. The experienced man of the world has become a blank sheet or *tabula rasa* (blank tablet/piece of paper), the phrase used by the Romantics to describe the utter innocence of the newborn child. The reader, however, knows that innocence and safety do not necessarily go together. The anxiety we might have felt for Walser when we did not know his immediate fate in the explosion is reawakened. How can a grown man with no knowledge even of how to feed himself, without any language or consciousness, survive in Siberia?

patronymic literally, the name of the father. Traditionally Russians are known by their Christian names, and an adapted version of their father's Christian name meaning 'daughter or son of'

CHAPTER 5   **The hostages have been kidnapped by outlaws and imprisoned in the middle of nowhere**

Meanwhile, the rest of the circus has been on a forced march through the Siberian forest. Fevvers limps along with her broken wing; and Lizzie is furious because she has lost both her handbag and her clock, the tools of

her magic. The march comes to a halt at the outlaws' encampment. The
hostages are treated quite well, given hot tea, vodka and cold meat, and
are shut into a shed with a fire and bearskins for rugs. They are worried
about the nature of their captors, especially when the boy outlaw who
tends the fire in the shed strangles one of the clowns' dogs. The Princess
of Abyssinia who has been unconscious up to this time awakes, in a
parlous state, like a sleepwalker, in the shock of having lost her piano and
her cats. Fevvers awakes the next morning to a message that the leader of
the outlaws wishes to see her alone.

The outlaw chief explains why he has captured the circus. The men
in the forest are all ex-prisoners brought to extremity by injustice. They
have blown up the circus train, knowing Fevvers was on it, because they
believe Colonel Kearney's false publicity that Fevvers is engaged to the
Prince of Wales. They have captured her to get her to intercede on their
behalf with Queen Victoria. When Fevvers explains that the newspaper
reports about her intimate relations with the royal family are lies, the
outlaw chief goes crazy, breaking up the encampment, and he has to be
restrained by Samson, who knocks him out. The captives are left to
wonder what will happen to them when he comes round. Lizzie, Fevvers
and the Strong Man hold a council of war. They consult Sybil as to what
they should do. She advises, using her alphabet cards, that they should
wait and see. The bandits are too drunk to feed their captives that night,
and Fevvers is beginning to despair, what with the loss of her sword and
the clock and her broken wing and her broken heart. Suddenly there is a
knock on the door. Someone asks for entry, and is invited to slip the bolt
and walk in.

> Now that the train has literally disintegrated, completing that
> movement away from structure and order hinted at in the anarchic
> performances of the clowns, the world of the circus has disappeared.
> Like Chapter 1 in this section, this chapter is narrated by
> Fevvers. Her style is that of the oral narrative, written as if it were
> being spoken, with all the digressions and tics of speech that this
> implies. Thus, although it is not immediately relevant to the matter
> in hand, Fevvers tells us explicitly that Lizzie's family are a bunch
> of 'anarchist bomb-makers' (p. 225), and Gianni, the ice-cream
> seller, was responsible for putting a real bomb in the *bombe surprise*

that killed the ex-whore Jenny's first husband. With Fevvers taking control of the story, there is now no objective voice that gives the events any sense of perspective, or that permits the reader a stable position from which to view them. If the circus was a topsy-turvy kind of world, the outer reaches of Siberia are all the more so. Here, the people in charge are outlaws; the usual rules no longer apply. In Petersburg, the circus at least performed in a context where its own excesses and anarchy were contained within and constrained by the world of conventions and normal expectation. The circus was licensed anarchy, and was therefore paradoxically predictable. In Siberia, Fevvers does not know what is going to happen and is consequently apprehensive. Her nerves show in her narrative by the digressions – the insistence, for example, that Lizzie is not a real witch, no matter how her actions appear (p. 225):

Now, when I call Liz a 'witch', you must take it with a pinch of salt because I am a rational being and, what's more, took in my rationality with her milk, and you could say it's too much rationality as procured her not altogether undeserved reputation, for when she puts two and two together sometimes she comes up with five, because she thinks quicker than most. How does she reconcile her politics with her hanky-panky? Don't ask me! (p. 225)

In this passage, the orality of Fevvers's narrative is obvious, in particular the ways in which it contradicts itself as only spoken language generally does. In that long sentence which both asserts that Lizzie is not a witch, and also suggests that she has a 'not altogether undeserved reputation' for witchcraft, there is a pull in two different directions. Similarly Lizzie's left-leaning materialist politics and her use of household magic ought to be incompatible. But they aren't, suggesting that she, like Fevvers, is a complex rather than a one-dimensional character. Like the question asked by Fevvers's publicity materials – 'Is she fact or is she fiction?' – Lizzie inhabits contradictions. Similarly, Fevvers is both a 'rational being' and a believer in Lizzie's 'hanky-panky'. This is not a world in which the binary oppositions of either/or structure understanding. This is a world of and/both: anything goes.

Despite the desperation of the situation, the broken wing, the loss of Walser and of Lizzie's clock and handbag, Fevvers remains feisty. Her indignation about the sexist assumptions of the outlaw leader shows her just as ebullient as she ever was. It also reiterates the doubled time frame of the novel as a whole. Fevvers's attitudes to women's liberation are the attitudes of the 1980s rather than those of the 1890s. As she suggests, she is not unsympathetic to the spirit of outlaws' aims for justice, but: 'the letter wants attending to here and there, to my mind. "Swords for sisters, rifles for wives," indeed! What kind of intercourse is that?' (pp. 229–30); or again, when the outlaw laments the 'dishonour' of his sisters and wives: 'Wherein does a woman's honour reside, old chap? In her vagina or in her spirit?' (p. 230). The narrow notion of a woman's honour as her chastity or virginity, common at the end of the nineteenth century, does not fit with Fevvers's view of the world – after all, she was brought up amongst honourable whores in a brothel, and is not averse to turning tricks herself for gain. The chief outlaw, as far as she is concerned, has a very outdated view of women, and even appears to be shocked that she uses a 'dirty' word like vagina.

Significantly in this context, of course, he has also misunderstood Fevvers's own position in society, led astray by Colonel Kearney's false publicity that the bird-woman is to marry the Prince of Wales (see Part Two, Chapter 7, p. 147). In the extreme landscape of Siberia, the relationship between cause (the news story) and consequence (the explosion) is played out in a very extreme way. Kearney, however, lacks any sense of responsibility for their plight. His whole philosophy is contained in the phrases: 'Never give a sucker an even break!' and 'Bamboozle 'em!' (p. 275); to his mind the outlaws are bamboozled suckers. He goes through no process of development in the novel; his whole attitude is based on the amorality of the profit motive. His only response to the situation is to get drunk on vodka and go to sleep. Only Fevvers, Lizzie, and the rapidly developing Samson the Strong Man are prepared to *take* responsibility, and to plan. Even Sybil's powers seem temporarily to have deserted her, since all she can recommend is that they wait and see. This is precisely what the reader will have to do. Knowledge of the future of the narrative is deferred, especially as the next chapter deals not with the hostages but with Walser's fate, so that the cliffhanger of a question – who enters the hut at the end of the chapter? – is not answered until later. Like Fevvers's narrative, the narrative as a whole tends to digress.

Jonah in the belly of the whale the Jewish prophet Jonah was swallowed by a great fish after a storm at sea, and lived for three days in its belly. See the book of Jonah, Chapters 1–2

dynamitards those who use dynamite, especially those who blow things up for political rather than practical purposes

My handbag it is possible that the importance of Lizzie's handbag is an allusion to Oscar Wilde's 1895 play *The Importance of Being Earnest* in which the plot revolves around the identity of a baby who was accidentally placed in a handbag, and then lost

'toot sweet' the Colonel's pronunciation of the French phrase *toute suite*, 'immediately'

Othello's occupation was gone in Shakespeare's *Othello*, Othello speaks the line 'Othello's occupation's gone' when he believes that his wife has been unfaithful to him. With his occupation (his love for his wife) gone, he has nothing left to live for. See *Othello* III.3.359

Swan and Edgar's fashionable department store in London's West End at the turn of the twentieth century

liberty, equality and fraternity the stated ideals of the French Revolution, though they were never realised by the revolutionaries. Fevvers objects particularly to fraternity (or brotherhood), since it seems to leave no place for women in the outlaws' plans

toper an indiscriminate drinker, a drunkard

Land of the Dragonfly Japan

Fidelio, by Beethoven the plot of the 1814 opera is loosely based on Shakespeare's *Twelfth Night*

Wagnerian Wagner's operas are famous for their tempestuous music

'caveat emptor' 'buyer beware', Latin proverb

false consciousness a technical term from Marxist theory, false consciousness is a system of illusory beliefs

Stephen Foster American songwriter (1826–64) whose lyrics tend towards the sentimental

by the water of Babylon they sit down and weep Psalm 137

CHAPTER 6   The amnesiac Walser is picked up by a Shaman

Walser is wandering around Siberia in the remnants of his clown costume. He has no memory. In the distance, he hears drumming. He pursues the sound of the drum and a sweet smell in the air until he comes across a Shaman in the forest, burning aromatic herbs and drumming as part of his mystical observance. The Shaman thinks that Walser is part of his hallucination. Walser settles down by the fire to warm himself. When the Shaman has finished his ritual he notices that Walser is still there, though he expects him to disappear at any moment. But Walser is hungry, and he remembers that when he rubbed his stomach before, the women from the House of Correction fed him, so he repeats the gesture. He is provided with a cup of fresh Shaman's urine which he drinks. It immediately gives him amazing hallucinations of his past life, though he can make no sense of them. Now the Shaman believes that Walser must himself be an inexperienced Shaman from another tribe. He picks him up in a fireman's lift and carries him back to his own village.

Walser began this novel being disoriented with a strange story and copious amounts of champagne. Now his disorientation is almost complete. He has no touchstone of normality to hold on to. All he has is his body and its needs: 'He is a sentient being, still, but no longer a rational one; indeed, now he is all sensibility, without a grain of sense, and sense impressions alone have the power to shock and to ravish him.' (p. 236). He is capable of feeling physical sensations but not of emotional affect or intellectual effort. When he had earlier glimpsed the 'humanity' of the apes and tigers, he had been shocked to realise their ability to feel and think. Now he is robbed of those abilities himself, reduced to being a bundle of physical needs, as helpless and innocent and ignorant as a baby. Like a baby – and, indeed, as with his only other previously remembered experience, being fed and petted by Olga Alexandrovna – he knows only the sensations of hunger and thirst. Now the quotation from *Hamlet*, 'What a piece of work is man!'

(p. 238), gains a new urgency. What does it mean to be a man if you are robbed of speech, memory, culture and civilisation, profession, clothing and self-consciousness? Where does Walser's humanity now reside?

Shaman medicine man or witch doctor, working cures by magic; priest of the religions of some parts of Northern Asia (including parts of Siberia)
Finno-Ugrian dialect Finno-Ugrian languages are spoken across the European and Asian areas of the Arctic circle and are notoriously difficult for Western Europeans to learn
fly agaric a poisonous mushroom used as a fly killer which also has the property of producing hallucinations; it is bright red with white flecks

CHAPTER 7   The captives meet the Escapee. The clowns dance up a whirlwind which carries them and the outlaws away. The remains of the party travel across the tundra to the 'Conservatoire of Transbaikalia'. There, they encounter the tribesfolk and spot Walser among them

The figure who had knocked at the door at the end of Chapter 5 was a newly arrived outlaw, an Escapee from Siberian exile. He had been sent to prison for an anarchist attack, and he and Lizzie are soon arguing about politics. Fevvers interrupts this discourse because she wants to know what will happen when the other outlaws come out of their 'gloom' (p. 240): the omens are bad and it's likely that the rest of the circus will be shot. In addition, the Escapee has news of Walser. He tells of having met up with the band of women from the House of Correction setting off to establish a female utopia in the Siberian wastes. They told him about Walser, whom they believe has been rescued by the relief train. Fevvers is very happy to discover that Walser is not dead. The Colonel perks up and begins to plan how he will capitalise on the story of the train wreck and the rescue.

The immediate problem for the circus refugees is how to escape being shot. Lizzie gets the clowns to entertain the outlaws so that they will forget their disappointment. The clown troupe goes outside to the outlaws' fire and begins its chaotic performance. They literally dance up a whirlwind which carries the clowns and the outlaws away. Only one mongrel dog remains. The last of the circus party decide to leave the encampment, and set off for the railway.

On their aimless wanderings they unexpectedly come across an isolated house with the inscription 'Conservatoire of Transbaikalia' written on the door (p. 245). They enter the house to discover decaying grandeur and a grand piano, at which the Princess miraculously awakes from her sleepwalking stupor. She is just about to rush up to it to play when the occupant of the house makes himself known, throwing himself in front of the instrument. There is a stand-off over possession of the piano, ended when Mignon begins to sing. The mad old man gradually starts to accompany her. For the first time ever the Princess speaks, commenting on the distressed state of the piano. The old man, Mignon and the Princess quarrel cheerfully over the repair of the piano while the others go and search for food. They end up eating the clowns' last dog.

The next morning, the old man shows them how to fish the frozen river; when they return to the house, the Princess has miraculously restored the piano, and is playing Mignon's song to accompany her. The sound is electrifying. It has drawn Siberian tigers from the woods, who have leapt on to the roof of the house, draping it like snow and icicles. It even seems to have brought the beginning of spring. The sound has also drawn the Shaman's tribe from their forest clearing, bringing Walser with them. Fevvers impetuously breaks the spell of the music, crying out to him; the tigers slink away. She tries to fly towards him, forgetting her broken wing, but the sight of her terrifies the woodsmen and they all disappear back into the forest.

This chapter begins with a political discussion couched in terms of a grammatical **analogy**: Lizzie berates the Escapee for his concern with a *future perfect* (the grammatical tense of 'will have been'); she argues that the present (the present continuous tense which describes ongoing situations) is imperfect because it is touched by the past historic (the tense of the narrative past which establishes the conditions of the present). We are about to discover from meeting the Shaman's tribe that this notion of past, present and future is not universal. For the time being, though, the circus party is definitely living in the present imperfect – stuck in the middle of nowhere with the imminent threat of execution which will annihilate their futures, perfect or not. But when Lizzie persuades the clowns to perform to entertain the outlaws, present and future take on a different character.

Even within the safe space of the circus ring, the clowns' performances have always been dangerous. (Buffo was nearly homicidal on his last appearance in the ring.) Without the structures of the circus to contain their anarchy, the clowns perform the ultimate dance of 'disintegration, disaster, chaos' (p. 242). They dance themselves and their audience of outlaws out of existence, the end point of the process that began with their first dance for Walser in Clown Alley. The first dance was disturbing because of its obscenity; this dance is disturbing because of its despair. Only the quick thinking of Samson saves Fevvers and the other non-clowns when he drags them to shelter: this is a sure sign of his development – who would have thought that Samson could be a quick-thinker?

At the Conservatoire, there is a different kind of enchantment, that of the Princess and Mignon's music. In this case, the release from the confines of the circus is a positive thing. The tigers who come to listen to the music are there through choice not coercion. Music, a highly structured art-form, brings order out of chaos, though it is still a strange kind of order. Mignon's singing has disordered the seasons and made the spring come early. The time of the seasons is disrupted, and so is the time of individual perception. When the woodsmen come out of the forest, Fevvers cannot recognise Walser, partly because of his clothes, but mostly because of his beard. She thinks that it is only two days since she has last seen him; but here the time is out of joint, and the winter is spring, and the journalist has grown a beard. When time came unhinged in the first part of the novel it was under Lizzie's control, with the help of her clock. Now they have no idea what time it is, or even what part of the calendar they are in. Indeed, they don't even know really *where* they are. Walser has lost his bearings in a very extreme way. But the rest of the party are lost too.

Utopia literally, 'No Place' (Greek); usually used to designate an ideal future state and its mode of government

Godwin and Wollstonecraft Debating Society William Godwin (1756–1856) and Mary Wollstonecraft (1759–97) were both writers associated with radical politics

Rodin's Thinker Auguste Rodin (1840–1917), French sculptor. *The Thinker* depicts a seated naked man, his head resting on one hand

eldritch weird or uncanny (Scots dialect)

George Buffins the real name of Buffo the Great, the deceased head clown

circles of hell in Dante's *Divine Comedy*, Hell (or *Inferno*) is divided into nine circles, each circle containing sinners of different kinds

tomorrows into yesterdays possibly an allusion to Shakespeare's *Macbeth*. On hearing the news of his wife's death, Macbeth speaks regretfully of the tomorrows that will never come and of the yesterdays that have led to death (V.1)

Old Adam in Christian and Jewish belief, Adam was the first man, and was the cause of subsequent sinfulness. Old Adam therefore refers to the view that human beings are inevitably fallen and sinning creatures

Kropotkin Prince Peter Kropotkin (1842–1921), Russian anarchist writer

denouement unfolding of the plot

shako tall, cylindrical, military hat

Shanks's pony to travel on foot (shanks being another term for legs)

Quixote ... Sancho Panza ... Dulcinea in Cervantes's picaresque novel *Don Quixote* (1605–1616), Quixote is a man in the grip of the powerful delusion that he is a knight from chivalric romance; Sancho Panza is his earthy peasant sidekick; Dulcinea is the imaginary lady he makes the object of his quest

Struwwelpeter literally, 'Shock-headed Peter', a character from German folk tale with long hair and nails: 'Struwwelpeter' is a warning to children against thumb-sucking

a capella without accompaniment

'Winter Journey' a song cycle by Franz Schubert (1797–1828), first published as the *Winterreise* in 1827

fearfully symmetric tigers burning as brightly an allusion to William Blake's poem, 'The Tyger' (from *Songs of Experience*, 1795): 'Tyger! Tyger! burning bright / In the forests of the night, / What immortal hand or eye / Could frame thy fearful symmetry?'

CHAPTER 8   Walser's life among the tribesfolk

The Shaman and his tribe treat Walser kindly as far as their own views of the world go. These views are strange to western eyes, since they focus on the idea that the world and dreams are continuous. Their system is complex, and has remained largely unchanged for centuries. The modern world has begun to impinge on theirs just a little. A Russian fur trader, for example, had infected the tribe with gonorrhoea, and the birth rate had dropped to an all-time low. And the steam train across Siberia had made some changes, bringing trade and firearms. But they are, in the main, untouched by 'progress'. In this world, Walser lives with the Shaman, his amnesia sanctified as a holy hallucination. The Shaman interprets all Walser's actions and words as signs of Walser's own progress as a Shaman.

In the Shaman's hut there also lives a bear cub destined to be sacrificed to the gods. Walser begins to learn the Shaman's language, but he dreams in English, which the Shaman interprets as the language of the astral plane. When Walser recounts a dream about a pig to the Shaman, the Shaman decides that Walser is to be the bear's executioner. He begins to prepare for the ceremony, firstly by getting a costume ready for Walser to wear, and then by preparing his disciple for becoming a Shaman himself by teaching him the tricks of the trade.

Walser now has a cloak made for him, covered in tin stars and stripes; with bells and feathers at his shoulders. He also has a drum. All that is needed to complete the outfit is a cap. To get inspiration for the cap the Shaman puts Walser on a reindeer on the day of the winter solstice and sets him off at random, followed by the entire tribe who are celebrating an unseasonably warm winter's day. As they travel towards the railway track they are intrigued by the sound of a woman's voice singing to a piano accompaniment. The tribesfolk are disturbed by the song; but as Walser approaches a house roofed with white tigers, something stirs in his memory. The Shaman is highly suspicious about this apparition, especially when the winged woman tries to fly towards them, but is shown to have useless wings that dump her in a snowdrift. When the tigers descend from the roof at the interruption of the music, the tribesfolk all melt back into the woods from whence they came.

It is difficult to decide the tone of this chapter, which describes the history and habits of the Shaman's tribe. At times the narrator is mocking the Shaman and his beliefs as self-indulgent and comically foolish. For example the Shaman's attempt to find a tree for Walser's drum, when the tree appears to say to him: 'Yah! Fooled you!' (p. 257). At other times, the Shaman's beliefs are clearly being compared (not necessarily unfavourably) with the practices of the capitalist world of the circus. When he teaches Walser the lessons of shamanism – the prestidigitation, ventriloquism and solemnity (p. 263) that are necessary to a good shamanistic performance – he is also teaching Walser the tricks of the circus magician. 'Seeing is believing' in this world as it is in the world of the circus (p. 263).

But the Shaman is not always right as is made clear by Walser's dream, narrated to the Shaman and comically misinterpreted by him:

'I see a man carrying a' – he fumbled for the word – 'a pig. You don't know what a pig is? A little animal, good to eat. The upper part of this man's apparel mimics the starry heavens. The lower part, by a system of parallel bars, represents, perhaps ... felled trees ... He brings light, and he brings food, but he also seems to bring ... destruction ...' (p. 261)

We know that this describes Colonel Kearney in his stars-and-stripes waistcoat (the US flag is mocked by the Shaman's attempt to replicate it in Walser's ceremonial clothes), carrying Sybil, but the Shaman understands Walser's dreams 'in his own way' (p. 262), as an omen that Walser should be in charge of the bear-sacrificing ceremony.

The Shaman's world is solipsistic: it refers only to itself and acknowledges no external reality. This is both comic and potentially tragic: funny because it is so far removed from our own sense of the world, but tragic because it is timeless. In the previous chapter, Lizzie had argued about the nature of time and grammar; her understanding of the world depends on ideas of past, present and future, mirrored in a language that can express those time frames. As a socialist, Lizzie certainly believes that the imperfect present could be bettered in the future, in particular by learning the lessons of the past. The Shaman's tribe, however, is timeless. 'They were a-historic. Time meant nothing to them' (p. 265). This is a parlous state of affairs, since timelessness implies the impossibility of change or development. The tribe's world is not perfect and they need to change or they will die out. As the narrative comments, they are dangerously crazy, 'intellectually speaking, permanently three sheets in the wind' (p. 253).

an instruction manual of universal knowledge of the 'Inquire within' type 'Inquire within' pamphlets were popular texts from which children (and adults) could amass factual knowledge from the late nineteenth century onwards

gonococci the bacteria that cause gonorrhoea

capercailzie woodland grouse

bruin the Dutch word for 'brown', Bruin has become an archetypal name for a bear (just as Fido is an archetypal name for a dog). The name appears in numerous children's stories and romances

seventy-four words ... for cold an allusion to the myth that the Inuit tribes of North America have as many as four hundred words for snow

Oh, say can you see / By the dawn's early light the opening words of 'The Star-Spangled Banner', the US national anthem

Yanqui Spanish form of Yankee, American

fourteen hundred and ninety-two the year in which, according to the old rhyme, Christopher Columbus 'sailed the ocean blue', and Europeans discovered the Americas

CHAPTER 9   **Lizzie and Fevvers decide to rescue Walser; Mignon and the Princess, and Samson stay at the Conservatoire to make sweet music with the Maestro; the Colonel and his pig set off with the Escapee with big plans for the future**

The Maestro of the Transbaikalian conservatoire tells his story. He was lured there by the promise of a glittering career teaching music to the children of the fur traders. The project never got off the ground, and he found himself stranded in the middle of nowhere with only a piano for company, just about succumbing to despair when the circus arrived. Since their arrival, he has perked up, delighted by his new pupils, Mignon and the Princess. Some of the group are finding happiness, but Fevvers is definitely disgruntled, in part because she is losing her looks, but also because she has lost her sense of invulnerability. And lastly, she is annoyed because Lizzie is not being cooperative in Fevvers's wish to rescue Walser.

Meanwhile, the Colonel is still planning how to make the most of the situation. The Escapee is so impressed by him that he decides to join the circus as Kearney's business manager when they all get back to the States. The problem appears to be that no one from the circus wants to go with the Colonel. Mignon and the Princess have decided to stay in Transbaikalia to study music. Samson wants to stay too out of unrequited, unselfish devotion to Mignon. And Fevvers refuses to follow him because she wants to rescue Walser. So the Colonel and his pig accompany the Escapee to the railway line without the rest of the circus.

A chapter about those who change and those who stay the same. Colonel Kearney is the same as he ever was – the caricature businessman with only profit in mind. But the other remnants of his circus have changed through their experiences. The Princess and Mignon have found happiness in their love for each other and their music. Samson decides to stay with them to serve them, which is what his strength fits him for; he has learned sensitivity. And Fevvers is ready to break her contract and lose her fee for the love of Walser: this from the woman who has twice nearly died for cash rewards.

one of Shakespeare's late comedies this might be a reference to either *Pericles, Prince of Tyre*, in which the Prince of the title loses and finally recovers his daughter, Marina, or to *The Winter's Tale*, in which the daughter, Perdita (meaning 'lost') is brought up by peasants and is only restored to her parents, Leontes and Hermione, at the end of the play

wot not of archaic form of 'know nothing of'

one of the ruins that Cromwell knocked about a bit music-hall song

New Woman topical reference to the 1890s. The term New Woman referred to emancipated women who sought professional careers, university education and the vote at a time when 'proper' ladies were supposed to be satisfied with marriage, motherhood and no franchise

For a pure heart becomes a cashbox best an allusion to, and a rewriting of Christ's Sermon on the Mount: 'Blessed are the pure in heart: for they shall see God.' See Matthew 5:8

sistren a play on the word 'brethren', meaning brothers. In Part Three, Fevvers objected to the outlaws' insistence on 'fraternity' since it omitted women. Mignon here redresses that balance

CHAPTER 10   Fevvers and Lizzie set out to find Walser

As Fevvers and Lizzie travel across the snowy wastes of Siberia, Lizzie lectures Fevvers about her morality, and about the folly of the attempt to rescue Walser. She wants to know the true motives for Fevvers's pursuit of the journalist: does she, in fact, envisage marriage with him as the proper happy ending for this story? Fevvers is shocked by this suggestion, though she argues in return that Walser is a malleable man, and can be moulded to whatever model of masculinity Fevvers chooses. Lizzie cannot see any profit motive in Fevvers's pursuit of Walser, and considers this a mark of her adoptive daughter's moral growth, though she notes dryly that it will be inconvenient for the financial health of the anarchist movement.

They are about to quarrel when they suddenly happen on signs of humanity. It is a primitive wooden hut in which a woman who has recently given birth to a child is lying, completely unattended except for her baby. Lizzie immediately takes control. They pick up the baby and the mother, and set off to find a better place for them to be cared for. As they leave the hut they come across an unseasonable crop of snow violets, a good omen. They follow the track to the woman's village.

Fevvers and Lizzie enter one of the buildings of the village with their human baggage. It is a room that stinks of blood and incense, but so ill-lit that they cannot see what is in there. After a few moments of silence a voice asks them what they are doing there. The mother shrieks and repossesses her baby and a fight ensues in the dark, with Lizzie wrestling with the Shaman's bear. Fevvers meanwhile fights an unseen assailant. When the lights come up she discovers that it is Walser whom she has defeated in battle. The Shaman is highly confused, and drums to try to exorcise the spirits who have interrupted his ceremony. Fevvers almost panics but Lizzie urges her to spread her wings, and like the true show woman that she is, she is revived by the arrival of an audience of villagers who come to see what is going on. The haze of Walser's shattered memory begins to clear. He asks her who she is and if she knows how to love. Fevvers, in full show woman's mode, replies: 'That's the way to start the interview! Get out your pencil and we'll begin!' (p. 291).

At the end of each of the two previous sections, Fevvers has been in mortal danger from predatory men. At the end of this section, that physical danger is repeated in slapstick mode, with a ridiculous fight in the village god-hut. The real danger to Fevvers in this chapter is what philosophers might call an **existentialist** crisis. Like Walser, Fevvers has also been deprived of all the touchstones by which she knows her own world and her own self. She is now dowdy with hair and feathers showing their natural colours. She has no role because she has no audience for which to perform. She is afflicted by a kind of nihilism – the belief in nothing, the denial of all external reality and all objective truth – as she journeys through the taiga:

the notion that nobody's daughter walked across nowhere in the direction of nothing produced in her such vertigo she was forced to pause and take a few deep breaths, which coldly seared her lungs. Seized with such anguish of the void that surrounds us, she could have wept (p. 280)

As Lizzie puts it, Fevvers is 'fading away, as if it was only always nothing but the discipline of the audience that kept you in trim' (p. 280).

Throughout the novel, Fevvers's problem has always been that she is both a real woman and a figure of fantasy, inhabiting mutually exclusive terms in a **binary opposition**. She is a symbol, a figure from the dreams of men, as well as being a solid material being with dreams and desires of her own, dreams which are often at odds with the pictures that others have of her. In her speeches to Lizzie in this chapter, she recognises her symbolic status, but tries to claim her symbolism for the cause of female emancipation; one day all women will have wings, she argues, and she will become 'no longer an imagined fiction but a plain fact' (p. 286). Lizzie, though, wants to keep Fevvers's feet, as it were, on the ground. Flights of fancy about a future world in which women are liberated will still have to contend with the messy facts of female biology – something emphasised by the fact that as they discourse on the future, in the present of the narrative they are dealing with a woman and her newborn baby. Lizzie, in other words, wants Fevvers to remember the female body and its functions. And when Fevvers is carried away with the idea of a happy ending in finding Walser, Lizzie reminds her that the happy ending depends on marriage, and implies maternity: 'I raised you up,' she says, 'to fly to the heavens, not to brood over a clutch of eggs' (p. 282). She argues that Fevvers must not sacrifice her uniqueness for the old-fashioned idea of love that has traditionally entrapped women.

The scene in the god-hut, with its comic fight, also has a more serious side for Fevvers, then. When the Shaman starts to 'exorcise' her:

Fevvers felt that shivering sensation which always visited her when mages, wizards, impresarios came to take away her singularity as though it were their own invention, as though they believed she depended on their imaginations in order to be herself. She felt herself turning, willy-nilly, from a woman into an idea. (p. 289)

In the scenes with Rosencreutz and the Grand Duke, that was also the nature of their threat to her. As with those previous occasions, it is only when she asserts her own uniqueness and refuses the Shaman's vision of her, as she had refused those other visions, that she takes control of the situation. For this she needs an audience, provided by the woodland tribe. Their belief reflects back on her performance, and makes that performance more powerful. And if the audience reinforces Fevvers's sense of her identity, her identity gives Walser back his: when she tells him to get his pencil out, she turns him back into a man ('pencil' must sound like a salacious word when Fevvers says it) and a journalist. The power of performance is stronger than that of 'authenticity'. Appearance *makes* reality.

syllogism logical argument consisting of two propositions and a conclusion that proceeds from the propositions. For example: 1. All Scotsmen wear kilts. 2. Angus is a Scotsman. 3. Therefore Angus wears a kilt

To travel hopefully is better than to arrive near quotation from Scottish writer, Robert Louis Stevenson (1850–94): 'To travel hopefully is a better thing than to arrive, and the true success is to labour', from *Virginibus Puerisque* (1881)

Orlando takes his Rosalind. She says: 'To you I give myself, for I am yours.' Orlando and Rosalind, the lovers in Shakespeare's *As You Like It*. The quotation is from V.4.IV

One footprint only, like Man Friday's in Daniel Defoe's *Robinson Crusoe* (1719), Crusoe discovers that he is not alone on the island when he comes across a single footprint in the sand

mind forg'd manacles from William Blake's poem 'London', *Songs of Experience* (1795)

The dolls' house doors will open a reference to Henrik Ibsen's play, *A Doll's House* (1879), a play about the enforced domesticity of women in late-nineteenth-century Europe

I see through a glass, darkly St Paul's first letter to the Corinthians, 13:12

vatic prophetic

ENVOI   As Lizzie solves the problem of low birth rates for the Shaman's village, Fevvers finally gets her man

Fevvers begins to explain to Walser. As she gets ready to go to bed with him, she tells him that Lizzie had to stop being a whore at Ma Nelson's because she insisted on making radical political speeches to her clients. She admits that they used Walser's diplomatic bags to send secret messages out of the country to anarchists in London; and she admits that they tricked him with Nelson's clock on the first night they met him. As she stands naked before him (and Walser notices that indeed she has no navel), he comes of age, and learns the meaning of love.

In another part of the village, Lizzie has taken charge of the mother and the newborn baby and is teaching the villagers the importance of post-natal hygiene. Her lessons will reduce the death rate in years to come.

Walser thinks about his own selfhood, and its relation to narrative, realising that he will have to start his character formation all over again. He asks Fevvers one last question: why did she try to convince him that she was the 'only fully-feathered intacta in the history of the world'

(p. 294)? And Fevvers is so delighted that she has managed to fool him that she does not answer, but laughs. Her laugh is enormous and fills the whole world.

Traditionally the 'envoy' of a poem or play is the writer's summing-up of events, his/her last word, or 'send-off' for the audience. In this case, the 'envoi' is inconclusive. Given the comic nature of the novel as a whole, and given that Lizzie in the previous chapter has insisted that marriage is the customary happy ending for a comedy (p. 281), and given also that there is much of the fairy tale about *Nights at the Circus*, marriage is perhaps what we should be expecting. In this case, however, what we get is a coupling without the benefit of a ceremony. The end is sex and laughter, both anarchic actions which subvert the convention of an ordered ceremonial. In addition, we get various kinds of confirmation of what we had always suspected – that Fevvers is not that kind of heroine anyway. Walser knows now that her feathers and wings are real; he sees for the first time that she has no navel; and in her bed, he discovers that she is not a virgin and so does not conform to the convention of the innocent heroine. The reader has always 'known' these things. But the confirmation of the journalist is significant because he began the narrative as a sceptical non-believer.

The change that has come over him is signalled by the two different brief narratives he constructs of his own life. The first is written in the manner of the journalist, full of facts and names that apparently authenticate the narrated events, and which ends with his marriage to Fevvers; the second is a more honest but less objective account, written with more exuberance, and concluded with the realisation that 'I shall have to start all over again' (p. 294). It is, of course, the second account that is more 'true' to the spirit of the novel. But their coexistence in Walser's mind suggests that his desire for Fevvers has made him move away from the either/or world of objective reality towards a more inclusive world view that allows him to have his cake and eat it too: Fevvers is all woman *and* all bird. The fact that she is not a virgin in either incarnation suggests her liberation from the old models of narrative (which must end with the virgin marrying the prince) and her emancipation from real-life models of femininity. And if Walser loves and desires her all the same, then he is a fitting New Man mate for her. No wonder she is laughing, though her laughter might also be at Walser's credulity: 'It just goes to show there's nothing like confidence' (p. 295).

Envoi the author's last words that send the audience on their way (from the French *envoyer*, 'to send')

the Irish question, the Indian question … all political questions on which Lizzie would have taken the radical point of view

'Habanera' from *Carmen* an opera by French composer Georges Bizet (1838–75), *Carmen* is the torrid story of a cigarette-factory girl and her tragic love for a soldier. The 'Habanera' is a quick-time dance from the opera, celebrating the good times before the tragedy unfolds

CRITICAL APPROACHES

CHARACTERISATION

The construction of character in *Nights at the Circus* can be seen on three different levels. There are the caricatures, exaggerated one-dimensional portraits; there are what might be called intermediate characters – that is, characters who at first appear to be caricatures, but who demonstrate the capacity to develop through the course of the novel. Finally, there are the major characters, Fevvers, Walser and Lizzie, who are complex from the outset, and who inhabit contradictions.

CARICATURE – COLONEL KEARNEY

The caricature figure shares much with what E.M. Forster called (in *Aspects of the Novel*, 1927) 'flat characters', figures motivated by a single idea and who are incapable of development. When we first meet Colonel Kearney, for example, we meet his whole personality mapped on his body and clothes. He is 'a little, fat man', balding, with a 'snub nose, and mauvish jowls', his colour being the result of copious consumption of bourbon whiskey. He wears 'a gun-metal buckle, in the shape of a dollar sign' to hold in his fat belly, and a stars-and-stripes waistcoat. 'Even in the relative privacy of his hotel suite, the Colonel sported his "trademark" costume' (p. 99). In that description, we actually have all we need to know of him: he is American, he drinks too much, and his only motivation is money. Those facts will condition his every action in the novel, and he will never show any development.

INTERMEDIATE CHARACTERS – SAMSON THE STRONG MAN AND MIGNON

The next order of character is those relatively minor figures who appear to be one-dimensional at the outset, but who demonstrate a capacity for change as the narrative progresses. An example might be Samson, the Strong Man, defined by stupid machismo at the beginning, but a character who learns sensitivity with the experience of unrequited love.

Another such character is Mignon, the abused child, the victim figure, who develops an autonomous subjectivity through her relationship with the Princess and the tigers, and her exposure to Fevvers. Mignon's story, told in detail in Part Two, Chapter 5, is like the case history a social worker or psychologist might narrate to explain the actions of a psychopath. Mignon's case history, with its catalogue of disadvantage – a murderous father, a life on the streets, thieving, begging, prostitution, work for a charlatan, and 'marriage' to a brutal drunken husband – would normally herald a life of impossible pain. Angela Carter, however, shows her creation transcending the conditions of her past. Mignon is given the capacity for happiness, demonstrating that an impossible childhood need not lead irrevocably to an adult life made only of pain.

MAJOR CHARACTERS – FEVVERS, LIZZIE AND WALSER

Finally, there are the complex major characters (or 'round characters') like Fevvers, Lizzie and Walser. These are figures who inhabit complexity and contradiction. Lizzie, for example, Fevvers's adoptive mother, is a rational woman, committed to anarchist politics because of her observations of the world around her. But she is also a kind of witch, able to manipulate the sense of time, to cause minor household disasters to those of whom she disapproves, a magic maker who keeps her magic in her handbag. Rationality and magic don't traditionally go together – but they do in Lizzie. From the outset, she lives with contradiction and accepts its consequences.

Walser, in contrast, is a sceptic who is brought to belief, who *learns* to inhabit these contradictions through the course of the book. He first appears as a handsome man of the world, but he has been untouched by experience. At the end of the novel, he recognises his own complexity, which has developed because of love. He separates himself from his mask of objectivity, and from his disguises as a clown and a journalist in order to discover 'what a piece of work is a man' when deprived of the props of civilised masculinity.

And, of course, there is Fevvers herself, all woman, but half bird: material girl, alleged virgin and tart-with-a-heart all rolled into one. Fevvers and Walser both have caricature touches about them at the outset – the material greed of the one, the practised disbelief of the other – but they both learn that there are other possible motivations for action. Fevvers also carries the burden of her feminine gender. She represents a whole series of cultural stereotypes about women. From the moment we meet her, a woman with wings, she literalises the slang term 'bird' for woman. Her legendary virginity, demanded by her culture for any respectable unmarried woman, is a fable that she tells herself, against the expectations of her society, not to support the ideal of the virgin, but to increase her market value. At the same time as appearing to be an ideal woman, a virtual goddess, however, she is also a powerful material force in the text. Her body is not ethereal or idealised at all. Instead it is filled with vulgar appetites, for food, sex, money and champagne. It is not the closed, hidden body usually associated with virginity. Rather it is a body placed on display, consumed by her audiences, and capable of grotesque actions as well as of marvellous feats. Her body houses a highly astute brain. Fevvers is a thinking woman as well as a feeling one. As such, she probes the stereotypes of her society, and shows them to be caricatures. Her complexity is her strength.

Nights at the Circus is set in the backstage environment of an exaggerated show-business world, and it concerns larger-than-life personalities, like Fevvers herself. But here, character is at least as much a performance as an expression of sincerity. Those who do not have potential selves behind their performing masks (the Colonel, the clowns, the Shaman) are displaced from the centre of the narrative in favour of those who can develop a character as well as a persona, the mere mask of public performance.

THEMES

REALITY AND ILLUSION

The most important theme of the novel is that of illusion and artifice and their relation to reality, a theme that pervades the whole text. Fevvers, for example, tells us very early that she dyes her hair and feathers: she's not a natural blonde, and her plumage is really dowdy. That kind of deception is expected and acceptable especially in a showbiz personality. But the confusion of illusion and reality is picked up in virtually all the settings of the novel. It's no surprise that the stage of a music hall is an illusion; nor that the circus ring is the setting for unreality, nor that performers fake their appearances through costume and make-up. But Nelson's brothel had only looked good in the half-light of 'deceitful candles' (p. 49); Gianni's ice-cream parlour looks innocent, but is actually a front for anarchist bomb-making; Madame Schreck's museum is in the respectable suburb of Kensington, but it's not a respectable enterprise; Rosencreutz's house has been built to look old, but is in fact new; the entrance of the Imperial State Circus is filled with the luxury of gilt and velvet, but inside it is grimy and pervaded by the scents of the performing animals. Petersburg itself, at least near Clown Alley, is filled with poverty, dead dogs and syphilitic prostitutes, though you would never know it from the way that Walser describes '*its boulevards of peach and vanilla stucco [which] dissolve in mists of autumn ...*' (p. 97). And this pervasive unreality taints the real, so that Fevvers on the Trans-Siberian train looks out at the tundra and sees it as a 'cyclorama, [an] unnatural spectacle' (p. 197) that looks like a theatre backdrop, so that the real takes on the attributes of illusion. The characters are constantly being unsettled by the mismatch between appearance and reality; readers are similarly upended. Seeing is never believing in this text, and we are deprived of our habitual tools to resolve narrative meaning.

HUMANS AND ANIMALS

The theme of appearance and reality is picked up and developed in the theme of man's relationships with animals in the novel, the theme of anthropomorphism (where animals are seen in human terms) which in turn raises the question of the meaning of humanity itself. When Walser observes the chimps at their daily schooling he is seeing one thing (the animals are rehearsing), and coming to realise quite another (the animals are doing something human). Similarly, he recognises the beauty of the tigress whilst having simultaneously to remember that she almost ate him: beauty resides in the beast in the case of the tiger; Walser might also be a beast within a noble human form. In other words, the novel insists that people are animals too, that they have bodies as well as 'souls' or spirits, and that those bodies with their physical needs condition our lives just as much as any higher faculty.

SOCIAL AND ECONOMIC CONDITIONS

The novel is thus also concerned with the materiality of existence, that is, the ways in which economic and physical conditions *form* personal experience and attitudes. What kind of life can a woman born with wings have? How do poverty and/or gender limit your choices? Examples include Fevvers's whole career, the life histories of the inmates at Madame Schreck's establishment, the story of Mignon, the life of Olga Alexandrovna, and the tableau of the baboushka with which the second section opens. All these characters are victimised by poverty and femaleness, though most of them also manage to escape their victim status.

The politics of the novel, with this concern for materiality, is related to both Marxism (the belief that man is an economic animal, that poverty conditions experience, and that poverty can be overcome) and feminism (the belief in female equality, the diagnosis of the causes of female inequality and suggested solutions for the problems it causes). Political commitment is central to *Nights at the Circus*, but it is not on the surface of the text. This is not a political treatise so much as a series of moral lessons in the necessity and possibility of changing people's lives. It is a comedy, and so the victims do generally escape to better lives, though the solutions to their problems are unlikely, to say the least. For example, Mignon's story is resolved in the Siberian tundra, in a musical conservatoire where she will study music with her lesbian lover. And the baboushka is sent Fevvers's diamonds, like a gift from a magical fairy godmother.

NARRATIVE STRUCTURE

TIME

The novel does not unfold in a straightforwardly chronological way. In part this is a function of the fact that it is a late-twentieth-century novel, set in the late nineteenth century. It is not, strictly speaking, a historical novel, however, since although it makes mention of real historical personages, and makes much of the flavour of the period in which it is set, it plays fast and loose with the conventions of history and historical narrative, which is usually seen as a sober chronicle of 'real' events. With the central figure here, a figure of fantasy, 'historical novel' does not describe the mode of narrative. Indeed, the narrator even tells us it must be obvious that this story does not belong to the 'violence of ... authentic history' (p. 97). Moreover, there are certainly occasions when the narrative deliberately makes it clear that it is written from a twentieth-century perspective. For example, the Sleeping Beauty is said to dream of the coming century, and her dreams are troubled by weeping (p. 86). This is the perspective of someone who knows that the century contains two World Wars, and various genocides.

That doubled perspective of 'now' and 'then' is replicated at different times through the text. Almost the whole of the first section, for example, is an extended analepsis (flashback). In the present of the story, Fevvers is a successful trapeze artiste, entertaining the press. But the story she tells is the story of her past life. The narrative moves between the time frames of present and past, taking the audience from the stifling dressing room to the various scenarios of Fevvers's autobiography and back again. A similar structure can be discerned in 'Petersburg', Chapter 5, where Mignon's story is told as a series of flashbacks from the present in Fevvers's hotel suite, while Mignon is singing in her bath. And it is also the structure of 'Siberia', Chapter 8, where Walser's life with the Shaman is narrated as flashback from the present of the narrative where Fevvers and the rest of the circus entourage are enchanted by Mignon's song at the house of the mad Maestro.

Repeating structure

The narrative structure also repeats itself in terms of the kinds of events that Fevvers lives through. One repeating structure is that towards the end of each section, Fevvers finds herself in serious danger, first with Christian Rosencreutz, then with the Grand Duke, and finally (and less seriously) with the Shaman in the inhospitable landscape of Siberia. In each case she escapes by behaving in a way her antagonist does not anticipate. This sets up the expectation that Fevvers will always escape, which is consistent with the novel's comic purpose. Another repeating structure is the way in which Fevvers deals in her storytelling with other characters she has met. In the first section, for example, we are introduced in detail to Ma Nelson's brothel, and when the brothel disperses, we get a pretty detailed breakdown of the fates of each of the girls. Similarly, the inmates at Madame Schreck's are also described and their tales completed. As the circus disintegrates in Siberia, the characters are disposed of, so that we know what happens to those we care about (i.e. we hear about Mignon and the Princess, but not about the clowns). Although this is, in many ways, a fairy-tale world, Fevvers's narrative does not dismiss her characters to the never-never world of 'happily ever after': she gives them all a specific future.

GENRE

The word **genre** means 'type' or 'kind' of writing. Its purpose is to give readers a horizon of expectation, a set of criteria against which they can judge the end result. If a text is comic, does it make you laugh? Is a horror story sufficiently scary? Does tragedy make you experience pity and fear? And so on. In the novel form, genre is an important consideration for readers, publishers and booksellers, since book-buyers tend to know what kind of book they like, and to return to that genre over and over again. One of the problems with (and one of the pleasures of) *Nights at the Circus* is that its genre is not entirely clear. It is obviously a comic novel, signalled from the outset by Fevvers's joyously exuberant character, and signalled at the novel's end by her laughter, spiralling like a tornado across the world. But it is not just 'a laugh'. There is more here than easy humour.

In an interview with John Haffenden, Angela Carter herself described the novel as **picaresque**, 'where people have adventures in order to find themselves in places where they can discuss philosophical concepts without distractions' (Haffenden, p. 87; see Further Reading). The picaresque is usually the narrative of the low-life rogue character who takes to the road and has lots of experiences. It is not conventionally a narrative mode suited to philosophy since the events happen so quickly that there is not the time to reflect on them; moreover, the rogue figure generally doesn't have the capacity for introspection. In this case, then, Angela Carter has taken the genre of the picaresque and used its setting for a more thoughtful purpose than is usual. Thus, characters do indeed ponder the nature of their own existence, do confront the meaning of life, in a way that the earlier models of this kind of writing did not allow.

If the novel is picaresque, then, it is not straightforwardly so. The picaresque may centre on adventure, but it does so in a resolutely realistic and everyday world. The world of *Nights at the Circus* is one in which elements of the fantastic intrude into everyday reality (Fevvers's very existence, for example, and her escape from the Grand Duke, and the enchantment of Siberian tigers by Mignon's song). As Haffenden commented, 'the term "magical realist" might well have been invented' to describe novels like *Nights at the Circus* (Haffenden, p. 76). Magic realism, as the term itself suggests, is a mixed genre in which the ordinary and the impossible coexist without apparent contradiction. This novel makes use of history, but is not a historical novel. It brings the traditions of fairy tale (where else does one meet a woman with wings?) and folk tale into the modern world of trains and telegrams. There are elements of science fiction (the Grand Duke's eerie automata) and elements of horror (Madame Schreck's museum). It is at once Gothic (Christian Rosencreutz's mansion) and comic (the mansion is an elaborate fake). Perhaps one way of describing it is as a postmodern novel, a text that borrows and remakes the conventions of earlier modes of narrative in a playful proliferation of styles. It is, however, important to pay careful attention to the interplay of different genres in the novel, and a useful exercise is to try to find an adequate generic label for some of the central scenes so that you can decide for yourself what the best description(s) of the text might be.

LANGUAGE & STYLE

Just as the genre of the novel is open to question, so its language compounds the confusion. The narrative is filled with abrupt shifts in register, from slang to technical language, from everyday conversation to high-flown philosophy. This tendency is marked from the very first page of the text, when Fevvers begins to speak in the language of innuendo ('for I never docked via what you might call the *normal channels*, sir' p. 7) associated with the music hall or stage cockney. But she is also capable of a more poetic mode.

> 'In Paris, they called me *l'Ange Anglaise*, the English Angel, "not English but an angel", as the old saint said,' she'd told [Walser], jerking her head at that favourite poster which, she'd remarked off-handedly, had been scrawled on the stone by 'some Frog dwarf who asked me to piddle on his thingy before he'd get his crayons so much as out sparing your blushes.' (p. 8)

In the space of a paragraph she moves from a reference to Pope Gregory to a much more vulgar reference to Henri de Toulouse-Lautrec, from angels to a 'Frog dwarf' in need of perverse sexual favours. This is a characteristic not just of Fevvers's language, but of the narrative as a whole. Fevvers's poster, for example, shows her 'bums aloft', from a 'steatopygous perspective' (p. 7): one a description in the vulgar vernacular, the other a highly technical medical term derived from Greek. The language refuses the conventional propriety of finding one register and sticking to it. It has a vertiginous effect, filled with unlikely juxtapositions and metaphors – a prison cell that looks like a rum baba (p. 211); a circus scene that resembles a painting by Breughel (p. 146); circus acts viewed as if they were the martyrdoms of saints (p. 120), and so on. Low culture sits in the context of high culture; the domestic and the official, the private and the public, become confused. The use of language is inventive and exuberant, matching the story it tells.

Another feature of the language of the text is its tendency to dramatise the action through typography and punctuation. Italics are liberally scattered through the text for emphasis. Ellipses and dashes punctuate the pauses. This is writing that actually owes much to orality, to the attempt to write narratives of the spoken word. Fevvers, the performer, not unnaturally has great comic timing in her delivery, a timing that comes from the oral tradition of the music-hall shaggy-dog story. The emphases and pauses in the typography mimic the stresses and gaps in spoken language, even when it is the narrative itself, rather than a character, that is 'speaking'. Another feature related to orality is that of the digression. In written language, one expects the argument or story to progress in a logical manner. But when we speak we often find it more difficult to stick to the point and can be waylaid by apparently irrelevant detail: was it Thursday or Friday, is she his sister or his sister-in-law?

Digression takes place in *Nights at the Circus* both on the large scale of the narrative structure as a whole (the discussion of the Siberian women's prison, for example), and in the small details of individual utterance (Fevvers's indiscretions about the proclivities of the 'Frog dwarf' quoted above).

The novel is written in this way not because Angela Carter knew no better. The mode of writing is connected to her political aims in the text. The language usage is inclusive (there are references that everyone might recognise) and expansive (there are references that you have to go and look up – you have to expand your knowledge to read it). In resisting conventional ways of writing and representation, Angela Carter was also resisting the conventional modes of behaviour that can fix people in unhappy lives. Fevvers is often disgusting: her table manners are vile, she burps and farts with abandon, she is so greedy for material things that she'll masturbate a Grand Duke if it furthers her purpose. She is in no sense a conventional novel heroine, demure, passive, petite and proper. In this world, though, if she were, she would die. If she behaved properly she would not be equipped to earn her living, and would not be able to escape the scrapes her fame gets her into. She is also likeable. Why would anyone choose a conventional biography with a prissy heroine, expressed in polite language over Fevvers's energetic narrative and *joie de vivre*?

SYMBOLISM

A symbol is something that stands for something else by conventional analogy. It differs from metaphor in that the meanings accrued to the object are broader than a single one-to-one correspondence. Thus the symbol of the rose might mean love, passion, pain, innocence, beauty and so on.

The figure of the winged human being is symbolic because of the multiplicity of its meanings. A winged woman might be an angel, a fairy, a Valkyrie, a cherub, a goddess, a representation of liberty, war, justice, mercy, death and love, amongst others. The bird woman also makes literal the colloquial metaphor of 'bird' used (usually derogatively) to mean woman. The multiple meanings that gather round Fevvers make her a living contradiction. The two pieces of music to which she usually performs neatly sum up two very different versions of the femininity she represents: 'I'm only a bird in gilded cage', a music-hall song for a working-class audience, that asks for pity and protection from them; and 'The Ride of the Valkryies', the high-culture music from grand opera, representing the winged woman as dangerous, fatal even, and as intensely powerful. Delicacy and potency coexist in Fevvers. She is never *only* a bird in a gilded cage. She spans the range of versions of femininity in her performance of herself. In the nineteenth century, a common view of femininity was that it existed only as two oppositions: women were either angels or whores. Fevvers disrupts the **binary opposition** of that version of femininity – she is both: a figure with wings brought up in a brothel. Sometimes she is a victim, sometimes an aggressor. But she is never fixed into either term of a binary opposition.

Lorna Sage has noted that the winged woman was a highly topical reference to the 1890s and early twentieth century. Using Marina Warner's important book *Monuments and Maidens* to ground her argument (see Further Reading), Lorna Sage shows that winged women were everywhere at the turn of the century, used as decorations for municipal statues of male war heroes (a winged Victory adorns General Sherman's statue in New York), as well as being used for commercial purposes: the winged woman 'settled on the bonnet of the Rolls Royce in the form of the Silver Lady, and (...) she turned up (gilded) on the Victoria monument in the Mall. She was already working as a logo, too, for Votes for Women, and as a cigar label.' (Sage, pp. 47–8). A winged victory figure celebrated conventional warlike masculinity; but a winged victory figure is also the representation of women's rights – hardly the same kind of symbol at all. She is adopted by high culture (statues to celebrate monarchy) and low culture (cigar adverts). These are all places where we might find Fevvers too. She's not averse to advertising; and she's not discomfited in any high-class scenario. She is a *cockney* Venus – both human and divine.

As Lorna Sage puts it, she is 'a symbol come to life *as a character*' (p. 48). The significance of that statement is that symbols, as Marina Warner argues, are very often embodied in female form, placed on pedestals and admired. Ideal femininity is a silent statue, virginal and still. But admiration comes at the price of autonomy. A symbol is an object, a thing that represents a virtue or a belief. That's a dangerous position for a real woman to find herself in. Pedestals are all very well, but they tend to be pretty narrow spaces, and it's very easy to fall off them. Fevvers's existence argues in contrast for a femininity that is full of life and movement, that is in charge of its own body and its destiny, and that makes its own meanings rather than having meanings imposed upon it.

Fevvers also perhaps represents the folklore figure of Mother Goose. Mother Goose is the teller of tall tales, stories that often combine the most mundane of experiences (hunger and poverty) with the most miraculous solutions to them: a gingerbread house to fill you up when you're starving, a beanstalk with a pot of gold at its top when you are destitute. At several points in the novel, Fevvers is her own narrator, and her voice is so powerful that it infects even those parts of the story where she is not speaking. The Mother Goose belongs in a realm of magic realism and speaks a language of both materiality and wonder. Fevvers carries the symbolism of the novel in her contradictory speeches, behaviour, actions and sensibility. She is a symbol because she represents so many things, contains so many possibilities, inhabits so many contradictions. She is the fairy godmother dispensing goodies to those who need them, the virginal angel of mercy, the madonna with the vile temper, *and* the tart with a heart.

PART FOUR

TEXTUAL ANALYSIS

TEXT 1   WALSER'S CHARACTER
(PAGES 9–10, PART ONE, CHAPTER 1)

His name was Jack Walser. Himself, he hailed from California, from the other side of a world all of whose four corners he had knocked about for most of his five-and-twenty summers – a picaresque career which rubbed off his own rough edges; now he boasts the smoothest of manners and you would see in his appearance nothing of the scapegrace urchin who, long ago, stowed away on a steamer bound from 'Frisco to Shanghai. In the course of his adventuring, he discovered in himself a talent with words, and an even greater aptitude for finding himself in the right place at the right time. So he stumbled upon his profession, and, at this time in his life, he filed copy to a New York newspaper for a living, so he could travel wherever he pleased whilst retaining the privileged irresponsibility of the journalist, the professional necessity to see all and believe nothing which cheerfully combined, in Walser's personality, with a characteristically American generosity towards the brazen lie. His avocation suited him right down to the ground on which he took good care to keep his feet. Call him Ishmael; but Ishmael with an expense account, and, besides, a thatch of unruly flaxen hair, a ruddy, pleasant, square-jawed face and eyes the cool grey of scepticism.

Yet there remained something a little unfinished about him, still. He was like a handsome house that has been let, furnished. There were scarcely any of those little, what you might call *personal* touches to his personality, as if his habit of suspending belief extended even unto his own being. I say he had a propensity for 'finding himself in the right place at the right time'; yet it was almost as if he himself were an *objet trouvé*, for, subjectively, *himself* he never found, since it was not his *self* which he sought.

He would have called himself 'a man of action'. He subjected his life to a series of cataclysmic shocks because he loved to hear his bones rattle. That was how he knew he was alive.

So Walser survived the plague in Setzuan, the assegai in Africa, a sharp dose of buggery in a bedouin tent beside the Damascus road and much more, yet none of this had altered to any great degree the invisible child inside the man, who indeed remained the same dauntless lad who used to haunt Fisherman's Wharf hungrily eyeing the tangled sails upon the water until at last he, too, went off with the tide towards an endless promise. Walser had not experienced his experience *as* experience; sandpaper his outsides as experience might, his inwardness had been left untouched. In all his young life, he had not felt so much as one single quiver of introspection. If he was afraid of nothing, it was not because he was brave; like the boy in the fairy story who does not know how to shiver, Walser did not know *how* to be afraid. So his habitual disengagement was involuntary; it was not the result of judgment, since judgment involves the positives and negatives of belief.

He was a kaleidoscope equipped with consciousness. That was why he was a good reporter. And yet the kaleidoscope was growing a little weary with all the spinning; war and disaster had not quite succeeded in fulfilling that promise which the future once seemed to hold, and, for the moment, still shaky from a recent tussle with yellow fever, he was taking it a little easy, concentrating on those 'human interest' angles that, hitherto, had eluded him.

This description of Walser's character occurs in the immediate context of his first meeting with Fevvers to whom the reader has just been introduced. We have discovered that Fevvers has an over-abundance of personality; she is considerably larger than life. And it is her experiences that have made her what she is, which is what the first section of the novel will demonstrate as her life story is told in great detail.

In contrast, Walser is here described in terms of what he is not, as an absence not a presence. The brief history we get of his life is very short of the 'checkable facts' that are his lifeblood as a journalist. There is nothing about his parents, his upbringing, his education: there is only his childhood dream of escaping to sea, given to us with no context except that he comes from California. His story, unlike Fevvers's (unlikely though her story is), lacks specificity. It is told, as it were, from a distance, as though it is impossible to be intimate with Jack Walser. He is a paradoxical thing – a character without characteristics: a shell, Lizzie calls him later (p. 171). The reference to *Moby Dick*, 'Call him Ishmael', even implies he is a character in disguise. In *Moby Dick*, it may well be that the narrator Ishmael is not really called Ishmael at all, but is travelling under a pseudonym. Since names are generally the reader's first point of contact with characters, Walser's resemblance to a man with a false identity is clearly significant. (Who is he to go round trying to explode Fevvers's reputation?) Moreover, *Moby Dick* is one of the great American adventure stories, concerned with defining American manhood in terms of dangerous action undertaken in extreme circumstances. It would seem that Walser has bought into a version of the American dream and has made himself in the image of a particular version of masculinity: 'He would have called himself "a man of action".' And, in the novel as a whole, he tries to live up to that ideal of heroism – for example, in his attempt to rescue Mignon from the tiger. The narrative, however, has little time for this brand of heroism, for the machismo of masculinity, as can be seen in Walser's humiliation after the tiger episode ('Petersburg', Chapter 5), or in the treatment of Samson, the Strong Man, before his development of sensibility.

Walser's experiences to date, then, are narrated with the kind of distanced objectivity that is associated with bad journalism. There is no emotion or detail attached to the list of things that have happened to him; it is just a list without any elaboration that would make the events seems real. He may have survived plague in China, spears in Africa, sexual assault in the Middle East; he may even have had experiences to rival those of Fevvers. But because 'he had not experienced his experience *as* experience', they don't make a good story: they are not interesting and they are not included in *this* narrative. In fact there is no trace of his experiences on him at all, no sign of the child he once was, no hint of what has happened since, under his very smooth manners. The metaphor of the 'handsome house that had been let, furnished', a house that looks good but is not really comfortable to live in because it lacks '*personal* touches' is an image that suggests that for Walser, surface is more important than content, illusion is more important than the reality. At the end of the novel, he diagnoses the problem of his character for himself: the things that happened all 'seemed to happen to me in the third person as though, most of my life, I watched it but did not live it' (p. 294). What he has lacked so far, is 'those "human interest" angles that, hitherto, had eluded him'. What he gets from Fevvers is 'human interest' in abundance – more detail, more emotion, more self-consciousness than he has ever experienced before. Instead of being an observer of life, he is made to become a participant. He moves from being an '*objet trouvé* ', from being a figure without a developed subjectivity, to someone who finds himself as a subject with his own desires and needs.

This introduction to Walser would usually be the treatment meted out to less important characters, those, perhaps, that the reader is not supposed to care about. He is not particularly sympathetic. He is just a blank to whom Fevvers is telling *her* story. His presentation is a caricature of banality. The point is, though, that he will change. From being a mechanical recorder of the chaos of other people's lives ('a kaleidoscope equipped with consciousness'), he will be forced to join in, hence his future role in the circus will be as a performer, not a backstage figure. At this point there is something inhuman about Walser which only the self-consciousness that comes from love will cure.

TEXT *2*   THE BABOUSHKA TELLS A STORY
             (PAGES 95–6, PART TWO, CHAPTER 1)

'There was a pig,' said the baboushka to Little Ivan, who perched, round-eyed, on a three-legged stool beside her in the kitchen as she blew on the charcoal underneath the samovar with a big pair of wooden bellows brightly painted with folk-art motifs of scrolls and flowers.

The toil-misshapen back of the baboushka humbly bowed before the bubbling urn in the impotently submissive obeisance of one who pleads for a respite or a mercy she knows in advance will not be forthcoming, and her hands, those worn, veiny hands that had involuntarily burnished the handles of the bellows over decades of use, those immemorial hands of hers slowly parted and came together again just as slowly, as in a hypnotically reiterated gesture that was as if she were about to join her hands in prayer.

About to join her hands in prayer. But always, at the very last moment, as if it came to her there was something about the house that must be done first, she would start to part her hands again. Then Martha would turn back into Mary and protest to the Martha within her: what can be more important than praying? Nevertheless, when her hands were once more almost joined, that inner Martha recalled the Mary to the indeed perhaps more important thing, whatever it was … And so on. Had the bellows been invisible, such would have been the drama of the constantly repeated interruption of the sequence, so that, when the old woman blew on the charcoal with the bellows, it could have been, if a wind had come and whipped away the bellows, a little paradigm of the tension between the flesh and the spirit, although 'tension' would have been altogether too energetic a word for it, since her weariness modified the pace of this imaginary indecision to such an extent that, if you did not know her, you would think that she was lazy.

And more than this, her work suggested a kind of *infinite* incompletion – that a woman's work is never done; how the work of all the Marthas, and all the Marys, too, all the work, both temporal and spiritual, in this world, and in preparation for the next, will never be over – always some conflicting demand will occur to postpone indefinitely any and every task. So ... there was no need to hurry!

Which was just as well, because she was ... almost ... worn out.

All Russia was contained within the thwarted circumscription of her movements; and much of the essence of her abused and withered femaleness. Symbol and woman, or symbolic woman, she crouched before the samovar.

The charcoal grew red, grew black, blackened and reddened to the rhythm of wheezing sighs that might just as well have come from the worn-out lungs of the baboushka as from her bellows. Her slow, sombre movements, her sombre, slow speech, were filled with the dignity of the hopeless.

'There was ...' puff! ... 'a pig ...' puff! 'went to Petersburg ...'

This passage comes from the opening of the 'Petersburg' section of the novel, and it helps to establish the strangeness of the place, providing writing with a significantly different pace and tone from what has preceded it. It also functions as an elaboration of one of the themes of the novel as a whole, the theme of the materiality of human existence. The novel consistently argues that the material conditions of any existence *form* the consciousness of the person who experiences those conditions, and this passage is a striking example of the argument being dramatised in the action.

At its simplest level, it merely describes an old woman blowing her fire to boil the samovar for tea. But the details of the description add up to much more than the simplicity of the situation they describe. The baboushka is old, inarticulate, weary and poor. She would also be pious if she were not so weary. The facts of her life, in other words, condition her existence. If she were not old and tired, blowing the fire would be easy. If she were not poor, then someone else would be doing this work for her.

If she lived a different life, she could afford an imagination, but she doesn't have the energy even to tell a proper story to her grandson. She is 'no Scheherezade' (p. 97) because her existence leaves no space for narrative fantasy. She is too tired to think and her weariness makes her situation appear inevitable to her. She has neither the language nor the time to analyse her situation, which makes it all seem eternal and unchangeable. As she bows before her fire, she looks like someone begging 'for a respite or a mercy she knows in advance will not be forthcoming'. This is a life of grinding poverty. Only the external observer who describes her movements can see a kind of poetry in them, watching the charcoal grow black and red; and even that is poetry of a rather grotesque kind since it expresses the futility of this existence. The motion of drawing her hands apart and bringing them together looks like a movement towards prayer, a prayer in the service of domesticity, so that the spiritual and the material seem to be combined in her action. Sadly for the baboushka, neither the spiritual nor the material demands of life will be met. Nor will the story about the pig ever be satisfactorily completed. In the final sentence, as elsewhere in the passage, "'There was ..." puff! ... "a pig ..." puff! "went to Petersburg ..."', the ellipses slow the pace of the prose, just as the baboushka's movements are also slowing. In addition, their interruption of the story shows how these physical tasks interrupt all thought, making it impossible even to imagine a different life.

The prose in which the baboushka is described is prose that is at odds with the scene it describes. It is a simple scene. But the narrative refuses to dismiss it in simple language, and insists on the importance of the kind of uncelebrated life that the baboushka leads. It pays attention to a figure who would normally be forgotten by other kinds of narrative. The baboushka's life is given an importance it would normally be denied, expressed in the parable of the opposition between Martha (domestic, hard-working) and Mary (spiritual). The narrative insists that the reader recognise the repetitiveness and tedium of her gesture as part of a *real* life, since real lives do tend towards tedium and repetition rather than excitement and adventure. The baboushka's tasks will never be over since there is always more tea to make. Like Martha, her materiality thwarts her spirituality. In the biblical story of Martha and Mary, Christ argues that Mary has 'chosen the better part'. The narrative implicitly criticises the idea that Martha has any choice in the matter at all. This is the order of everyday reality from which the circus represents a break. But people like the baboushka never get to go to the circus.

Having said that, of course, a whole book about her might not be much fun to read, especially if presented as a situation for which no solution is proposed. The baboushka's life is one of the reasons for Lizzie and Fevvers's socialism – this is what they propose as the solution to the problem of poverty, though the revolution will probably come too late for the baboushka, and when it comes, it might not solve anything. So, when they leave Petersburg, their last act is to relieve her poverty – Fevvers throws the Grand Duke's diamonds at Little Ivan who has been forcibly removed from the train, and tells him to give them to his granny (p. 193).

TEXT 3   FEVVERS ESCAPES FROM THE GRAND DUKE
(PAGES 191–2, PART TWO, CHAPTER 11)

Down below, the mechanical musicians continued to play and the ice continued to melt.

She gathered together her scattered wits as well as she could and moved resolutely on to the next case, continuing to manipulate him as she did so, as if her life depended on it. He dragged his feet, growing so blissful he scarcely noticed her open the case with her free hand.

And, here, inside a silver egg criss-crossed by a lattice of amethyst chips, she found, to her incredulous delight, nothing less than a model train – an engine, in black enamel, and one, two, three, four first-class carriages in tortoiseshell and ebony, all coiled round one another like a snake, with, engraved on the side of each in Cyrillic, the legend *The Trans-Siberian Express*.

'I'll have that one!' she cried, reaching in greedily. Her exclamation and sudden movement roused the Grand Duke from the trance she had induced, although she never stopped caressing him; she'd not served her apprenticeship at Ma Nelson's academy for nothing.

'No, no, no,' he forbade her, although his voice was glutinous with tumescence. He weakly slapped the hand that held the train but she did not let go. 'Not that one. The *next* one's for you. I ordered it especially. They delivered it this morning.'

It was white gold and topped with a lovely little swan, a tribute, perhaps, to her putative paternity. And, as she suspected, it contained a cage made out of gold wires with, inside, a little perch of rubies and of sapphires and of diamonds, the good old red, white and blue. The cage was empty. No bird stood on that perch, yet.

Fevvers did not shrink; but was at once aware of the hideous possibility she might do so. She said goodbye to the diamond necklace down below and contemplated life as a toy. With oriental inscrutability, the automatic orchestra laid down the geometrics of the implausible and, by the thickening of his member, the movements that now came of their own accord, by his panting breath and glazed eye, Fevvers judged the Grand Duke's time was nigh.

Then came a wet crash and clatter as the ice-carving of herself collapsed into the remains of the caviare in the room below, casting the necklace which had tempted her amongst the dirty supper things. The bitter knowledge she'd been fooled spurred Fevvers into action. She dropped the toy train on the Isfahan runner – mercifully, it landed on its wheels – as, with a grunt and whistle of expelled breath, the Grand Duke ejaculated.

In those few seconds of his lapse of consciousness, Fevvers ran helter-skelter down the platform, opened the door of the first-class compartment and clambered aboard.

'Look what a mess he's made of your dress, the pig,' said Lizzie.

The weeping girl threw herself into the woman's arms. It was the dark abyss of the night, into which moon plunges. In this abyss she had lost her magic sword. The station master blew his whistle and waved the flag. The train, slowly, slowly, began to pull its great length out of the station, dragging with it its freight of dreams.

This passage comes from almost the end of the 'Petersburg' section. It describes the outcome of Fevvers's encounter with the Grand Duke, his plan to keep her in a miniature egg as a toy, and her magical escape from the situation. This is the most spectacular of several instances in the novel when magical events overturn the apparent realism of a given situation. It narrates how Fevvers comes to the realisation that the Grand Duke's intentions towards her are highly dangerous. Immediately before this passage begins, he has discovered and broken her sword, and she has realised that he wants to shrink her and turn her into an object in his collection of Fabergé eggs. She thwarts this intention by using her skills as a prostitute to distract his attention; and she escapes by jumping on to a miniature train from another egg, arriving dishevelled and tearful in her own first-class compartment on the Trans-Siberian express.

The whole atmosphere of this chapter has been one of strangeness and obscure danger. The Grand Duke's house is filled with luxurious objects that are also somehow threatening, including the ice statue of Fevvers herself, and the orchestra of automata that provides the background music to the scene. Fevvers is already spooked by this encounter, not least because it has become clear to her that she is not in control of it. In other tight spots – like her encounter with Christian Rosencreutz ('London', Chapter 5) – she has been physically and mentally tougher than her opponent. The Grand Duke is much more powerful. He has broken the sword that surprised Rosencreutz, and he has her in a room with no windows, so there is no avenue for escape as there was last time this happened. Her only weapon in this situation is her sexual skill, her ability to manipulate sexual desire to her own ends. She continues throughout the scene to 'manipulate him (…) as if her life depended on it' (which, of course, it does). The Duke is so distracted by her expert touch that 'he scarcely noticed her open the case with her free hand'. This is the sleight of hand of the magician, which distracts attention from the real event. In other words, Fevvers is engaged in a rather sordid conjuring trick. This trick has been played on her already, since her motivation for coming to the encounter is material greed – the Grand Duke has used her weakness for diamonds and jewelled eggs against her to distract her from his purpose. Now she plays the trick in reverse, using his sexual weakness against him.

The staging of the scene is a play on the word 'climax' which can refer to both narrative excitement and sexual orgasm. The description of 'a wet crash and clatter' depends on that double meaning – it is in fact the ice statue melting, but it also refers to the Duke's ejaculation which is almost simultaneous with this. But the final transformation of the scene, from Grand Duke's apartment to compartment on the Trans-Siberian train, occurs without logical explanation. Like the Duke, the reader has been tricked: now you see it, now you don't. Unlike magic in more conventional narratives though, this magic doesn't do away with the material consequences of its action. When Fevvers gets to the train, she is in a bad way, weeping, her dress torn and covered in semen. This is an instance of magic realism, not just because of the movement from reality to fantasy, but also because the magic does not dispense with the reality of what has just happened to the heroine. She is not untouched by her experience, reappearing bandbox fresh; rather she carries the evidence of experience on her body and clothes.

The language of the passage typifies Angela Carter's technique. It mixes the registers of poetry with those of slang. The egg that has been prepared for Fevvers, for example, has a perch made of rubies, diamonds and sapphires – 'the good old red, white and blue' of the Union flag. The value of the materials contrasts incongruously with what they represent; the flag is usually a pretty cheap product, and 'the good old red, white and blue' is pretty ordinary language for extraordinary materials. Or again, the creepiness of the automaton music with its 'geometrics of the implausible' is the background sound to the melting of the ice statue into 'the dirty supper things'. Elevated thought and language coexist with slangy expressions and straightforward prose, just as, in the scene as a whole, the setting of magnificent opulence is at odds with the material greed and the possessive acquisitiveness of the two protagonists, and with the masturbatory sex that Fevvers performs on the Duke. The incongruities of the language mirror the incongruities of the action.

PART FIVE

BACKGROUND

THE AUTHOR AND HER WORKS

Angela Carter was born Angela Stalker in 1940 in Eastbourne, just as the Dunkirk evacuation was getting under way. Her parents lived in London – her father was a journalist, her mother a housewife – but because of the Blitz, she spent the war in South Yorkshire with her mother and maternal grandmother, returning to London when the hostilities were over. She was educated at a local primary school and the grammar school in Balham. When she left school her father arranged for her to become a junior reporter on the *Croydon Advertiser*, assuming that she would 'work her way up' through the ranks to a post in Fleet Street. Instead, Angela Stalker married Paul Carter in 1960, and moved away from London and her journalistic career to follow her husband's job.

After a couple of years of being a housewife, Angela Carter enrolled at the University of Bristol to read English as a mature student. She specialised in medieval literature, an interest that can be traced in her fiction writing in her emphasis on oral traditions, allegory, magic, fantasy and the bawdy. Her first novel, *Shadow Dance*, set in a city very like Bristol, was published in 1966. The action takes place in a Gothic world of 1960s fakery, and it narrates a nightmare vision of mutilation and murder. Her second novel, *The Magic Toyshop*, tells the story of three orphaned children left in the care of a powerfully malevolent uncle, Philip, a toymaker and owner of the toyshop of the title. He manipulates the children and the rest of his family as if they are just toys in his own terrifying playroom, before the toyshop is destroyed in a cataclysmic scene and the children are released to make new lives of their own in the shadow of their desperate experiences. This text, published in 1967, won the John Llewellyn Rhys prize for fiction, and was later turned into a television film. *Several Perceptions* (1968) tells the story of Joseph, a young man living amongst a community of hippies and drop-outs and struggling to come to terms with the twentieth century's barbarity in the context of the Vietnam War. It argues for alternative ways of seeing (the several perceptions of the title), and ends relatively happily, despite the carnage of the war, with various degrees of reconciliation to fate amongst the characters. It won the Somerset Maugham Award for literature, and with the money from that prize, Angela Carter went to Japan, first for a visit, and then to live until 1972. Her experiences in Japan were published in articles for the *New Statesman* magazine, and have been reprinted in her collected journalism, *Shaking a Leg* (1998).

Heroes and Villains, which came out in 1969, is a science fiction dystopia, set in a post-nuclear age, when the world is divided between Professors (lovers of order), Barbarians (nomads) and Out People (radiation-damaged mutants). It tells the story of a Professor child, Marianne, who sets out to join the Barbarians, but discovers that they do not represent the freedoms she had sought. The novel ends with her decision to stay, nonetheless, after the deaths of her tormentors, and to rule Barbarian society herself. *Love* (written in 1969, published in 1971) presents a more naturalistic world in which a ménage à trois between a wife, a husband and the husband's brother ends in the wife's suicide. But with *The Infernal Desire Machines of Doctor Hoffman* (1972), Angela Carter returned again to science fiction and fantasy. The novel is set in an imaginary South American country where a mad scientist has made machines that make desires come to life. It tells the story of how rationality more or less defeats this crazy science as the 'hero', Desiderio, sets out on a quest to reassert the values of the common-sense world. This is one of the novels on which Angela Carter's reputation as a magic realist resides. Also in 1972, Angela Carter was divorced from her husband. The collection of short stories, *Fireworks* was published in 1974.

Angela Carter's interest in fakery and illusion resurfaces in *The Passion of New Eve* (1977), a story about the illusions of the silver screen, involving a man who becomes a woman, and a screen goddess who turns out to be a man in drag, amongst other things. This novel also produces a very dystopian version of American life, as the 'hero/heroine', Evelyn confronts the brutal realities played out on female bodies in dysfunctional societies. Like almost all her previous books, it is a text about perversion, and about the abuse of power in sexual relationships. It's no surprise, then, that Angela Carter's most sustained non-fiction work, *The Sadeian Woman: An Exercise in Cultural History*, commissioned for Virago and published in 1979, is a meditation on the meanings of the Marquis de Sade's works in contemporary culture, and a consideration in particular of the two female figures on whom he centres so much attention: Justine, the passive victim, and Juliette, the enthusiastic participant in orgiastic pleasures. Angela Carter much prefers Juliette – and in *Nights at the Circus* (1984) you can see that passivity leads to victimhood; it is the powerful woman who makes her own way. *Nights at the Circus* also shares some of the atmosphere of the fairy tale, in which Angela Carter had become increasingly interested from the mid 1970s. Her collection of short stories, *The Bloody Chamber* (1979) is a rewriting and reinvention of several well known stories into different forms, often with very different endings. In particular, the princess figure does not always wait passively to be rescued; sometimes she rescues herself, sometimes she is the aggressor, and on one occasion, her mother shoots the villain for her, showing that Angela Carter was interested in rewriting the genre to reflect many possibilities of female personhood. One of the stories, 'The Company of Wolves' was adapted by Angela Carter and Neil Jordan for the 1984 film of the same name. Through the seventies, Angela Carter had continued to work as a journalist for *The New Statesman* and other publications, and she had been a writer in residence at the University of Sheffield, then, in the early 1980s, in the United States at Brown University, Rhode Island. She taught creative writing at the University of East Anglia, and was a member of the editorial advisory board for the newly formed Virago Press.

By 1984, when *Nights at the Circus* was published, Angela Carter had settled in South London with a new partner, and had had a son (1983). For the rest of the 1980s, she wrote journalistic pieces and taught at various universities in the States. In 1991, *Wise Children* was published, another look at the showbiz world, this time through the eyes of two seventy-five-year-old former dancers and showgirls who take us on a whirlwind tour of popular and highbrow British culture through the twentieth century.

Angela Carter died from cancer in 1992.

HISTORICAL & LITERARY BACKGROUND

Nights at the Circus, of course, has two different orders of historical background. There is the world of the end of the nineteenth century and the new beginning of the twentieth; and there is the context of the period in which the text was written, the 1980s. There is a sense in which the 1890s are not imagined as a historical period, however. There are lots of 1890s details, lots of references to real figures from the period (Toulouse-Lautrec, Willy and Colette, Alfred Jarry); allusions to others (August Morel, Isaac Merritt Singer); imitations of real figures, such as Colonel Kearney's resemblance to Phineas T. Barnum. Angela Carter herself argued in an interview with Anna Katsavos that the novel does have a historical dimension. It is set, very deliberately, at the turn of the nineteenth century, at a time when things were changing, in particular for women; Angela Carter said that Fevvers was a New Woman, and: 'All the women who have been in the first brothel with her end up doing those "new women" jobs, like becoming hotel managers and running typing agencies' (Katsavos, p. 13, see Further Reading). And yet at the same time, the novel also abounds with conscious anachronisms: quotations from poems that have not yet been written (there are two examples from W.B. Yeats, where the reference to 'The Circus Animals' Desertion' [p. 69] and to 'The Second Coming' [p. 117] refer to texts written in 1939 and 1919 respectively); there's the knowledge that the hopes for the twentieth century will be disappointed figured in the Sleeping Beauty's weeping, or the prediction of the Russian Revolution in the part of the narrative that describes St Petersburg. So although there appears to be an authentic period flavour, this, like much else in the novel, is a skilful simulacrum.

This historical 'unreliability' relates very much to the literary history of the period in which the text was written. Indeed, it might be viewed as one of the defining characteristics of postmodernism. It is a device to be found in novels such as John Fowles's *The French Lieutenant's Woman* (1969), Günther Grass's *The Tin Drum* (1959) or Salman Rushdie's *Midnight's Children* (1981): all make use of a narrative or narrator carefully placed in history, but also divorced from it. In her interview with John Haffenden, Angela Carter denied that there was any direct influence from writers such as these in her conception of *Nights at the Circus*. It is, on the other hand, clear that the traditional straightforward narratives of history seem to have become inadequate to express a certain kind of fiction for many writers after the Second World War. Angela Carter herself argued that she was influenced more by fairy stories and folklore, by medieval literature, with its complex allegories and fantastic settings and events, and by literary fiction's need to see itself as a mode of entertainment. 'I don't mind being called a spell-binder,' she told Haffenden. 'Telling stories is a perfectly honourable thing to do. One is in the entertainment business' (Haffenden, p. 82).

But entertainment is not her sole purpose. The purpose of debunking so-called sacred truths is a moral purpose. Angela Carter is anxious not to let us think that current injustices are normal, natural and inevitable. When she attacks the myths of our culture, she is seeking to *change* the conditions in which those myths arise. For a writer with socialist and feminist credentials writing in 1984, this must have felt like an urgent political task, since Britain was then governed by the Conservative Party under Margaret Thatcher. For leftist women, Mrs Thatcher was not a heroine, partly because of her general politics, but also because of her views about women's social position which were paradoxically old-fashioned. Angela Carter was certainly influenced by the women's movement, and it's no accident that she was one of the figures associated with the founding of the feminist publishing house, Virago Press. One of the contexts for her own writing therefore is that of other politically committed women writers. The Canadian novelist and poet Margaret Atwood with her analyses of the psychic effects of gender on women; Toni Morrison and her consistent concern with the material basis of race, gender and economic oppression on Black Americans of both sexes; and even Fay Weldon, whose commitment to causes is often difficult to pin down, but who shares Angela Carter's irreverence for sacred cows; these women and others, if not direct influences on her writing, are part of the background in which that writing takes place.

Working as a reviewer for several publications, the range of Angela Carter's reading was eclectic to say the least. She wrote about pornography, reviewing the porn-star, Linda Lovelace's autobiography and George Bataille's *The Story of the Eye* as well as the works of the Marquis de Sade. She covered a large range of contemporary fiction, from science fiction (J.G. Ballard) to magic realism (Jorge Luis Borges, Gabriel García Màrquez and Salman Rushdie, whom she passionately defended after the passing of the Iranian death sentence against him).

She was a member of the judging panel for the Booker Prize in 1983. She reviewed collections about Hollywood cinema, history, anthropology, cooking and travel writing, all of which are relevant to *Nights at the Circus*. Tracing a single line of influence is therefore impossible in the case of Angela Carter. Her works are a collage of concerns and genres which reflects a remarkable breadth of interest.

PART SIX

CRITICAL HISTORY & BROADER PERSPECTIVES

RECEPTION AND CRITICAL HISTORY

(Details for all references are given in the Further Reading section.)

The first reviews of the novel were largely very positive, enthusiastic for the exuberance with which the text was written, and for the larger than life heroine. Valentine Cunningham in *The Observer* saw it as both 'freaky and sinister' and as relishing 'black but also puckish comic turns'; he wrote that it was a 'stunning novel' which was both amusing and serious. Gillian Greenwood (*Literary Review*) called it 'a glorious enchantment (…) rooted in an earthy, rich and powerful language'. And Adam Mars-Jones (*Times Literary Supplement*) described 'a glorious piece of work, a set-piece studded with set-pieces'. Other reviews and interviews reiterated this praise in the same kind of language.

It is unusual for a book published relatively recently to have had so much written about it. Since her early death, however, there has been an enormous interest in Angela Carter's work. Lorna Sage, for example, notes in her introduction to *Flesh and the Mirror* that in 1992–3, more postgraduate students wanted to write doctorates on Angela Carter's works than on any other single subject in twentieth-century literature. Her death completed her writing so that one could look at the *whole* work and comment on its coherence or otherwise. There were also memorial collections of essays (*Flesh and the Mirror* is one such), which commented on, and celebrated, Angela Carter as both personality and writer.

But in the mass of material that has been generated, there are few easily identifiable strands of common criticism. *Nights at the Circus* is often given a literary-historical genealogy – a set of antecedents that somehow explain how it works; but from essay to essay, as Sarah Bannock has argued, the search for sources might be an exhausting and meaningless exercise. She sees elements of different kinds of biography at work in Fevvers's story; in contrast, Isobel Armstrong argues that *Nights at the Circus* is the inheritor of a female tradition that originates in Virginia Woolf's fantasy novel *Orlando*. And Marina Warner situates Fevvers in the realms of fairy story and Hollywood fantasy. For Lorna

Sage, Fevvers is a symbol come to life, a material goddess. Paulina Palmer argues that the text embodies polyphony and intertextuality, speaking with many voices and quoting liberally from, or alluding promiscuously to, a vast range of possible sources. In other words, the only critical consensus is that the novel is worth reading, that it has literary value and that it expresses moral values – though what those moral values are is not always easy to say. It is probably too soon for a critical consensus to emerge, and given the plurality of the novel, it may never do so.

CONTEMPORARY APPROACHES

Because Angela Carter was herself so well read in contemporary cultural theory her writings are almost textbook performances of contemporary critical concerns. The three types of reading offered here certainly do not exhaust the possibilities. In fact, they only refer to the most obvious critical positions that the novel invites.

BAKHTIN AND FOUCAULT: CULTURAL THEORY IN ACTION

The word 'culture' has many different meanings. In everyday language, it tends to refer to highly valued artistic products such as poetry, painting, sculpture, classical music and literature more generally. In this definition, a cultured person would be one who understood and valued Beethoven and Shakespeare, Dickens and Van Gogh. In literary theory and criticism, however, this view of 'culture' has been superseded by a more inclusive definition. A culture is a people's (a tribe's, a nationality's, a group within in a larger group's) 'whole way of life'. Cultural theory involves the study of the intersections between different parts of human life, from comic books to prison systems, from popular film to patterns of work, from individual family life to the entire economic basis of a society. Such theories do not regard painting or literature as necessarily more significant than soap operas or advertising. Rather, culture takes place on a continuum between the so-called 'highest' forms that belong to an educated elite and those belonging to ordinary people, often called 'low' or 'popular' cultures.

Nights at the Circus dramatises this more inclusive notion of 'culture' in its structure and plot. Its setting, backstage in the popular entertainments of the circus and the music hall, is the world of 'low' culture. At the same time, though, high cultural references abound. Fevvers, for example, has two signature tunes, one from music hall ('I'm only a bird in a gilded cage') and one from grand opera ('The Ride of the Valkyries'). She may have been brought up in the working-class atmosphere of an East End brothel, but: she also knows enough philosophy to recognise Christian Rosencreutz's sources; the brothel contained a large collection of books and a picture by Titian; she was a regular at performances of Shakespeare in Battersea ('"We dearly love the Bard, sir," said Lizzie briskly. "What spiritual sustenance he offers!"' p. 53); and she consorts with the Prince of Wales as well as with Lizzie's family of ice-cream makers. Fevvers's culture is very inclusive indeed.

The Russian writer Mikhail Bakhtin coined two terms that describe the processes at work in the novel. He wrote about the literatures of the carnivalesque, in which the authority of official or 'high' culture is destabilised and mocked. The idea of the carnival is that it is a time of licence and revelry, often associated with Christian festivals such as Twelfth Night, Halloween and Mardi Gras, or with pagan festivals such as May Day and Midsummer's Eve. These are times when the profane (over-indulgence in pleasures of the flesh, drunkenness, fornication and general disorder) is placed in the context of the sacred (Christ's birth or crucifixion). He argued further, that a literature of carnival is dialogic or polyphonic, meaning that it contains many voices and many registers. Such a literature does not settle on one version of truth, but allows multiple possibilities to coexist in constant play with each other. This has the result of making carnivalesque literature open-ended. It is not conclusive and closed, with all the loose ends neatly tied up. In *Nights at the Circus*, although different parts of the story are closed (for example, the fates of the inhabitants of Madame Schreck's museum are all neatly listed), the novel as a whole has an open structure. Fevvers and Walser are still stuck in the middle of nowhere at the end; we have no idea how, or even if, they are going to get home; we are simply left with Fevvers's laughter, itself a sound from the carnival. There is no final resolution.

In other words, *Nights at the Circus* is structured on competing discourses or language practices. From the individual level of the sentence to the structure of the novel as a whole, the dialogic is on the surface of the text. It is a comic novel with serious undercurrents running through it. If 'culture' means 'a whole way of life', then everything is up for grabs. In the novel, one of the places in which the dialogic nature of culture is played out is in the contrasting spaces of the circus ring and the prison, which are both part of the 'whole way of life' of Russia at the end of the nineteenth century. The circus ring is the space of creative disorder in which the usual hierarchies are disrupted. The audience sees wild animals behaving as cultured beings – the tigers listen to music and the apes go to school – and it also sees human beings acting the goat – the clowns are anarchic and the trapeze artistes defy the laws of gravity. This disorder, however, takes place in a contained space. The anarchy doesn't really break the rules unless it spills outside the performance area. Once the carnival is over, anarchy is shown to be only temporary. Order is reimposed. At moments when the dividing line between the circus space and the world beyond it is unclear (as it is in the case of the Great Buffo), the threat of anarchy becomes real and terrifying.

A prison, on the other hand, is a place dependent on rules and order. As such, the introduction of the panopticon prison in Siberia must appear at first as a textual aberration in the novel. But it is not a random introduction. Indeed, Angela Carter was committed to the idea that novels don't *just* tell stories, but that they also elaborate philosophies as they do so. She told John Haffenden that 'The female penitentiary (...) is where I discuss crime and punishment as ideas' (Haffenden, p. 79). In addition, in reflecting on a space committed to absolute order, the panopticon prison is also in dialogue with that other circle, the circus, informing and modifying the view of what goes on in the world of entertainment by reflecting on what goes on in the world of crime and punishment:

> It was a *panopticon* she forced them to build, a hollow circle of cells shaped like a doughnut, the inward-facing wall of which was composed of grids of steel and, in the middle of the roofed, central courtyard, there was a round room surrounded by windows. In that room [the Countess would] sit all day and stare and stare and stare at her murderesses and they, in turn, sat all day and stared at her. (p. 210)

That description is itself dialogic, combining the hardness of the steel grids with the soft shape and homely metaphor of the doughnut into a single image. The conflation of architecture and confectionery on the small scale of the individual description is mirrored in the conception of the novel as a whole.

This idea of the prison is almost certainly derived from French philosopher, Michel Foucault's book *Discipline and Punish: The Birth of the Prison*, in which the structure and purpose of the panopticon are described in detail. Michel Foucault argued that the panopticon differed from the dungeon because its purpose was to prevent concealment whereas the dungeon was constructed to hide the prisoner away. 'Visibility is a trap', he wrote (Foucault, p. 200); its purpose was to prevent misbehaviour by ensuring that any action by a prisoner could potentially be seen and then punished by the prison authorities. Michel Foucault's larger argument is that the ways in which societies punish their criminals directly correlate with the wider views of that culture in general. By extension, Angela Carter argues that the ways in which a given society entertains its people are similarly an expression of that society's larger values. The circus and the prison share both a context (they are in the same novel) and a geometry (they are the same circular shape). We are invited to read them as connected structures, and our expectations about their meanings (prisons bad, circuses good) are subverted, though not evenly so – our expectations are not simply overturned because, in the end, both prisons and circuses are shown as bad, in different ways and for different reasons. The clowns appear more unnatural and perverse than the murderesses. The world of entertainment has more serious and disturbing implications than the world of the prison. The prison and the circus are both significant functions within culture, implying a wide definition of the word in the novel, and suggesting its dialogic nature, its refusal to close narrative possibilities by providing the reader with authoritative answers.

MARXIST APPROACHES

Marxist approaches to literature are a very diverse group of writings with a broad range of interests and approaches. There are, however, some general characteristics that Marxist theories share.

The first is the critique of capitalism. That is, all Marxist approaches mount a criticism of the economic system of the West in which the profit motive is the ultimate arbiter of all action. *Nights at the Circus*, in its caricature of Colonel Kearney in his stars-and-stripes waistcoat with a dollar sign for a belt buckle dramatises that critique. Because of his monetary greed, Kearney is not an attractive figure. In addition, it is a sign of Fevvers's moral growth when she first undertakes an action without a view to profit when she goes off into the wilderness to find Walser. Through the novel, the monetary basis of life is consistently shown to be degrading and destructive, leading to prostitution and exploitation, amongst other evils.

The second general characteristic of Marxism is that Marxist critics are politically motivated to improve the conditions of the real world beyond the text. It is not so much that Marxists see literature as a series of revolutionary writings that will bring about world socialism; rather, the critique of capitalism that Marxist critics undertake when they read literary texts is a diagnosis of the wider picture of society in general. This is connected to a third characteristic of Marxist criticism: Marxists argue that the relationships between literature and society are so interwoven that one should describe literature as a social discourse. Literature and other artistic forms are inevitably social because they are produced and disseminated in the social contexts of a given society. What a writer is able to imagine is directly related to the material, economic, social and general cultural factors of his or her society. Literature does not offer 'spiritual sustenance' as Lizzie puts it ironically in relation to Shakespeare, so much as opportunities for the analysis of historically specific social circumstances of the text's production and reception. Marxism is a materialist approach to the text: it views the literary artefact as arising from and reflecting a set of material conditions.

In *Nights at the Circus*, the actions that characters undertake are more often than not the result of economic constraints. Women do not become prostitutes through choice, but through necessity, Fevvers tells us when she explains how she ended up in Madame Schreck's museum. Little Ivan's baboushka is entirely circumscribed by the material and economic conditions of her life. But these conditions are neither natural nor inevitable. They have been caused by history, and the people of the present in the novel have it in their power to change the world. As Lizzie puts it:

'It isn't in that Grand Duke's nature to be a bastard, hard though it may be to believe; nor does it lie in those of his employees to be slaves. What we have to contend with (...) is the long shadow of the *past historic*, (...) that forged the institutions which create the human nature of the present in the first place.

'It's not the human "soul" that must be forged on the anvil of history but the anvil itself must be changed in order to change humanity. Then we might see, if not "perfection", then something a little better, or, not to raise too many false hopes, a little less bad.' (p. 240)

In other words, human nature itself is not 'natural'. The Grand Duke of course prefers conditions in which he remains privileged, but that is not a matter of human nature. Rather it is the result of whole histories of exploitation and slavery which have left him in a position of privilege, and which have disenfranchised his serfs to the extent that they believe that their slavery is natural. Change the conditions in which people live, however, and it will be possible to change the nature of 'human nature'. It is perhaps for this reason that the central figure of the novel is a freak of nature, the anomalous winged woman. Fevvers is already so different that she calls the very notion of human nature into question. She represents the possibility of different lives embodied in her own physical difference. The lives that she touches – especially the lives of Mignon and Walser – are irrevocably altered by her contact with them. Fevvers is a one-woman revolution. On her own, though, she cannot alter the whole unjust system; she can only tinker with parts of it, and make individual lives better – the baboushka gets the diamonds, but what about all the other baboushkas? Her story demonstrates the necessity of more far-reaching reforms of economic and political systems.

FEMINIST APPROACHES: ÉCRITURE FÉMININE

Like Marxist approaches, feminist forms of criticism are very diverse, and there are several points of overlap between Marxism and feminism. Like Marxism, feminist theory is a materialist theory, largely concerned with physical, economic and social conditions. Like Marxism, it is always concerned with connecting the written word and the world beyond the text, seeing literature as intrinsically social. And like Marxism, its aim is to diagnose the problems of an imperfect present with the ideal goal of making the world a better place. But where Marxism begins from the assumption that economic conditions are the key elements in social and psychic formations, feminist theories always consider the oppression of women based on the fact of their gender as the key to their analysis. They might look at economics as well, but the position of women within a given economic system is their prime concern. Materialist feminism, the concern for women's economic deprivation and victimisation, is clearly at the heart of *Nights at the Circus*. The women of Fevvers's early life are prostitutes out of economic necessity; but they are prostitutes also because they are women – there is a market for their services which men desire and can pay for, and which women do not desire and could not afford in the context of late-nineteenth-century culture.

One of the criticisms levelled at both Marxism and feminism when they approach texts from the point of view of the analysis of content is that such approaches do nothing to account for the 'literariness' of the text. In other words, just looking at the story is not an adequate response to a text that has formal characteristics worthy of analysis as well. For this reason, both feminist and Marxist theory have developed theories of language and form that emphasise the political implications of literariness. Mikhail Bakhtin, discussed briefly above, was a Marxist as well as a cultural theorist, and argued that the dialogic structure of carnivalesque literature was political because it demonstrated the possibility of alternative social formations through language and form as well as through content.

The French feminist theorist Hélène Cixous approaches the question of literariness from the issue of gender. She argues that Western thought has tended to be structured by binary oppositions, that is, terms like white and its opposite black, man and woman, sun and moon, intellect versus feeling. In all of those oppositions, she says that the first term is traditionally more valued than the second (white is better than black, etc.), and that when one examines this structure, one discovers that each opposition could be rewritten in terms of gender: all of the positive terms are associated with man, all the negative ones with woman. Thus in Western cultures, masculinity means strong, intelligent, active, public and independent; femininity means feeble, sensitive, passive, private and dependent. These are the cultural values ascribed to each sex, not their natural attributes. But only when the diagnosis has been made can steps be taken to undo this structure which always privileges male over female. She recommends a process of *écriture féminine* (female/feminine writing) as one possible method for mounting an assault on the common assumptions about men and women that actually entrap and limit both sexes.

Almost everything about *Nights at the Circus* could be understood in terms of the destabilising, subversive effects of *écriture féminine*. For example, the novel's very genre, with its mixture of fantasy and realism, unsettles the binary logic that says that reality is more important than magic. Fevvers herself dramatises the undoing of binary oppositions. She is a real woman, but she also has real wings – a biological impossibility who actually exists in the world of the text. Both her characterisation and that of Walser demonstrate how the stifling assumptions of binary thought can be unsettled for radical ends. Walser, for example, begins the novel as a 'real man', a culturally powerful man of the world; but he is reduced during the text to a man who wears make-up and frilly clothes when he is disguised as a clown, rendering his gender status uncertain. He spends part of the novel performing as a human chicken, losing his identity as a man in the process. And he wanders through the Siberian wasteland having lost his memory and his language, signalling a very tenuous grip on his humanity. At the same time, Fevvers is not always properly feminine. She is physically large (not diminutive like a 'proper' heroine); she is physically voracious, eating and drinking with gusto (no anorexic appetite here). She demonstrates that femininity is often just an illusion, held together by big hair, powerful scent, hair dye and make-up. And she claims to be a virgin not for reasons of morality, as with the conventional feminine heroine, but for reasons of commerce: her legendary inaccessibility makes her more marketable, despite the fact that her virginity is highly unlikely.

Thus neither Fevvers nor Walser is fixed in a particular gender identity. Equally, other characters have traces of cultured attributes of the opposite sex. The Strong Man, for example, appears as a figure of extreme machismo, but he cries like a baby when Mignon rejects him. And characters who are fixed in their gender identity are in a lot of trouble. The absolute passivity of the Sleeping Beauty may be perfectly feminine, but it will be the death of her. The Grand Duke is another macho man whom we never see develop. He is not an attractive figure, though, as though Angela Carter is arguing that gender identity ought to be unstable. That's where the fun comes from in life.

Angela Carter's writing style partakes of excess. She makes reference to every area of cultural life from the highest to the lowest, and scrambles the reader's ability to categorise. The writing itself, as well as its larger structures of plot, makes mockery of order and makes the reader laugh in the process. It is laughter that should be seen as political, undoing the structures of oppression, as Fevvers's tornado of laughter does at the end of the novel; but it should also be seen as pleasurable because in this kind of writing, pleasure and politics are not in opposition.

FURTHER READING

SELECTED CONTEMPORARY REVIEWS

Valentine Cunningham, 'High-Wire Fantasy', *The Observer*, 30 September 1984, p. 20

Gillian Greenwood, 'Flying Circus', *Literary Review* 43 (October 1984), p. 43

Adam Mars-Jones, 'From Wonders to Prodigies', *Times Literary Supplement* 4252 (28 September 1984), p. 1033

Robert Nye, *The Guardian*, 27 September 1984

STUDIES OF ANGELA CARTER

Joseph Bristow and Trev Lynn Broughton (eds), *The Infernal Desires of Angela Carter: Fiction, Femininity, Feminism* (Longman, 1997)

> In this collection see especially Clare Hanson's '"The red dawn breaking over Clapham": Carter and the Limits of Artifice'; Sarah Bannock's 'Auto/biographical Souvenirs in *Nights at the Circus*'; and Paulina Palmer's 'Gender as Performance in the Fiction of Angela Carter and Margaret Atwood'

Aidan Day, *Angela Carter: The Rational Glass* (Manchester University Press, 1998)

Sarah Gamble, *Angela Carter: Writing from the Front Line* (Edinburgh University Press, 1997)

John Haffenden, *Novelists in Interview* (Methuen, 1985)

Anna Katsavos, 'An Interview with Angela Carter', *Review of Contemporary Fiction* (14, 3, Fall 1994), pp. 11–17

Lorna Sage (ed.), *Flesh and the Mirror: Essays on the Art of Angela Carter* (Virago Press, 1994)

> In this collection see especially Marina Warner's 'Angela Carter: Bottle Blonde, Double Drag' and Isobel Armstrong's 'Woolf by the Lake, Woolf at the Circus: Angela Carter and Tradition'

Lorna Sage, *Angela Carter: Writers and their Work* (Northcote House, Plymouth, 1994)

GENERAL BACKGROUND

Mikhail Bakhtin, *Rabelais and his World*, trans. Helene Iswolksy (Indiana University Press, 1984)

> This is the volume in which Bakhtin elaborates the concept of carnival

Hélène Cixous, 'Sorties' in *The Newly Born Woman*, written with Catherine Clement, trans. Betsy Wing (Manchester University Press, 1986)

> See this volume for the working out of the concept of *écriture féminine*

Angela Carter, *Shaking a Leg: Collected Journalism and Writings* (Vintage, 1998)

> Angela Carter's collected journalism is good to dip into to get some sense of her breadth of reading and interests. Helpful background for *Nights at the Circus*

Michel Foucault, *Discipline and Punish: The Birth of the Prison*, trans. Alan Sheridan (Penguin, 1977)

> See this book for the description of the cultural meaning of the panopticon

Rosemary Jackson, *Fantasy: The Literature of Subversion* (Methuen, 1981)

> Useful for thinking about the politics of anti-realist writing

Brian McHale, *Postmodernist Fiction* (Routledge, 1994)
> Introduces concepts around postmodernism that might be useful for thinking
> about Angela Carter's techniques and strategies

Lorna Sage, *Women in the House of Fiction: Post-War Women Novelists*
(Macmillan, 1992)
> Places Angela Carter in the context of other contemporary women writers

Richard Todd, *Consuming Fictions: The Booker Prize and Fiction in
Britain Today* (Bloomsbury, 1996)
> Places Angela Carter in the context of contemporary British literary fiction in
> general

Marina Warner, *Monuments and Maidens: The Allegory of the Female
Form* (Vintage, 1996)
> Describes in detail the cultural and historical meanings of the winged woman

World events		Angela Carter	Other writers
Silver Jubilee of Queen Elizabeth II	**1977**	*The Passion of New Eve* (novel) published	*Fire on the Mountain* by Anita Desai
Virago Press publish their first independent title			*Song of Solomon* by Toni Morrison
			Aunt Julia and the Scriptwriter by Mario Vargos Llosa
Louise Joy Brown becomes the world's first 'test-tube baby'	**1978**		*The World According to Garp* by John Irving
			The Sea, The Sea by Iris Murdoch wins Booker Prize
			Praxis by Fay Weldon
General Election – Margaret Thatcher becomes Prime Minister	**1979**	*The Sadeian Woman: An Exercise in Cultural History* (non-fiction) published	*If on a Winter's Night a Traveller* by Italo Calvino
		The Bloody Chamber (short stories) published and wins Cheltenham Festival of Literature Award	*Shikasta* by Doris Lessing
First CND rally at Greenham Common, Berks, against proposed siting of US Cruise missiles	**1980**	Visiting professor in the Writing Program at Brown University, Rhode Island	*Winter Garden* by Beryl Bainbridge
			The Middle Ground by Margaret Drabble
			Rites of Passage by William Golding wins Booker Prize

World events		Angela Carter	Other writers
Prince of Wales marries Lady Diana Spencer	**1981**		*Lanark* by Alasdair Gray

The Comfort of Strangers by Ian McEwan

Midnight's Children by Salman Rushdie wins Booker Prize |
| Falklands War | **1982** | *Nothing Sacred* (journalism collection) published | *On the Black Hill* by Bruce Chatwin wins Whitbread Prize for best first novel

The 27th Kingdom by Alice Thomas Ellis

The Color Purple by Alice Walker |
| General Election – Conservative Party voted in again | **1983** | Angela Carter a member of the judging panel for the Booker Prize

Birth of Angela Carter's son | *Life & Times of Michael K* by J.M. Coetzee wins Booker Prize

William Golding wins Nobel Prize for Literature

Waterland by Graham Swift |
| Miners' strike begins (ends 1985) | **1984** | *Nights at the Circus* is published | *Flaubert's Parrot* by Julian Barnes

Hotel du Lac by Anita Brookner wins Booker Prize |

World events		Angela Carter	Other writers
	1984	Film of *The Company of Wolves* with Neil Jordan	Ted Hughes appointed Poet Laureate
			Small World by David Lodge
Live Aid concert for Ethiopian famine relief	**1985**	*Nights at the Circus* wins the James Tait Black Memorial Prize	*The Handmaid's Tale* by Margaret Atwood
		Black Venus (short stories) published	*Oranges are Not the Only Fruit* by Jeanette Winterson wins Whitbread Prize for best first novel
Chernobyl explosion at Ukrainian nuclear power station releases large quantities of radiation	**1986**	Publication of the anthology *Wayward Girls and Wicked Women* edited by Angela Carter	*A Perfect Spy* by John Le Carré
General Election – Conservatives re-elected	**1987**		*And Still I Rise* by Maya Angelou
			Moon Tiger by Penelope Lively wins Booker Prize
			Beloved by Toni Morrison
Lockerbie Pan Am jumbo blown up above Scottish borders; 281 die	**1988**		*Oscar and Lucinda* by Peter Carey wins Booker Prize
			Where I'm Calling From by Raymond Carver

World events		Angela Carter	Other writers
	1988		*Utz* by Bruce Chatwin
			The Satanic Verses by Salman Rushdie
Tiananmen Square killings in China	**1989**		*Cat's Eye* by Margaret Atwood
Demolition of Berlin Wall begins			*The Remains of the Day* by Kazuo Ishiguro wins Booker Prize
Ayatollah Khomeini pronounces 'fatwa' on Salman Rushdie			*The Cloning of Joanna May* by Fay Weldon
Violent demonstrations in London against the poll tax	**1990**	Publication of *The Virago Book of Fairy Tales* edited by Angela Carter	*London Fields* by Martin Amis
Mrs Thatcher resigns; John Major becomes Prime Minister			*Possession* by A.S. Byatt wins Booker Prize
Gulf War	**1991**	*Wise Children* (novel) published	*Immortality* by Milan Kundera
			The Famished Road by Ben Okri wins Booker Prize
General election; Conservatives re-elected	**1992**	*Expletive Deleted* (journalism collection) published	*The English Patient* by Michael Ondaatje wins Booker Prize
		Angela Carter dies, aged 51	

allegory (from the Greek for 'speaking otherwise') a story that can be interpreted in two or more coherent ways. Allegory was a particularly important method for understanding medieval literature, where the ostensible story on the surface often partially concealed a series of other religious and moral meanings

anachronism (from the Greek for 'out of its time') the inclusion of an action or object in a work of art or literature which is out of time with the historical period being depicted

analepsis (from the Greek for 'to take back') a flashback

analogy (from the Greek for 'equality, proportion') a parallel, or a point of comparison

antagonist (from the Greek for 'struggle against') the chief opponent or enemy of the hero/heroine (the protagonist) in a story

anthropomorphism (from the Greek for 'the shape of a man') the attribution of human qualities to animals or inanimate objects

bathos a ridiculous movement from elevated language and treatment, or from heroic events, to ordinary dull language and everyday events. Bathos is one of the effects of juxtaposition

bawdy writing which is lewd or sexually explicit. Bawdy is often found in medieval literature

binary opposition the fundamental contrasts (such as in/out, off/on, good/bad) by which language itself operates. Language and the concepts it describes are relative; we only know that something is 'good' because we have access to the opposite term 'bad', and to relative terms like 'better' and 'worse'. In other words, binary oppositions structure the ways that we think in foundational ways

caricature a grotesque or ludicrous rendering of character, achieved by exaggeration, usually for comic or satirical purposes

carnival, carnivalesque (from the Latin for 'a farewell to flesh') a term first used by the Russian critic Mikhail Bakhtin to describe the ways in which some writers use their works as an outlet for the spirit of the carnival, of popular festivity and misrule. The carnivalesque can be understood as a politicised form of writing because it overturns the culture of the ruling classes, undermining the claim of the elite to have a monopoly on either morality or culture defamiliarisation a term derived from Russian formalist writers in the 1920s, defamiliarisation refers to the ways in which writing can 'make things strange' so that ordinary events, people or places have to be considered anew

deferral putting off resolution. This can occur in the midst of a narrative, when the reader is kept ignorant of what happens next for some time. Or it can refer to the whole tenor of a narrative which refuses to settle all the outcomes of the plot at the end of the story

dialogic dialogic texts allow the expression of a variety of points of view, and do not set out to resolve the conflicts of the different perspectives. The word was coined by Mikhail Bakhtin, and can be used to describe the literature of the carnivalesque

dystopia (from the Greek for 'bad place') an unpleasant imaginary world, the opposite of a utopia

écriture féminine a term coined by the French critic Hélène Cixous. It literally means 'female/feminine writing' and describes the ways in which authoritative forms of written language can be rewritten, subverted and deformed for the political purposes of feminism

existentialism (noun), existentialist (adjective) a philosophical theory that emphasises lived human experience as the basis for all action

fairy tale, folk tale usually originating as oral narratives, fairy tales and folk tales tell stories about fantastic or magical events

feminism (noun), feminist (adjective) the political belief in the equality of women with men in all spheres of life, including the material, the psychic and the intellectual

genre (noun), generic (adjective) (from the French for 'type' or 'kind') the term of a type or kind of literature, referring first to the major divisions of writing – drama, prose, poetry – then to subdivisions within those larger categories. The importance of genre is that it gives readers a horizon of expectation, a set of criteria against which to judge the piece before them. Novels might belong to genres such as romance, horror, science fiction, thriller and so on. A horror novel is judged by how frightening it is, a thriller by the element of suspense it generates

Gothic Gothic fiction is a genre that depends on a gloomy, obsessive, sometimes violent and usually frightening atmosphere. It concentrates on bizarre events and on strange physical and psychological phenomena

hubris (noun), **hubristic** (adjective) (from the Greek for 'insolent pride') overweening pride; in Greek tragedy, hubris was the fatal flaw that brought the hero low

hyperbole (from the Greek for 'throwing too far') extreme exaggeration

innuendo (from the Latin for 'to nod or wink at') an indirect reference, often to something smutty or vulgar

intertextuality a term invented by the French critic Julia Kristeva to refer to the kinds of different relationships that exist between texts within any given piece of writing. Julia Kristeva suggests that all writing operates by processes of adaptation, translation, allusion, quotation or parody of other texts

irony (noun), **ironic** (adjective) (from the Greek for 'dissembling') irony consists of saying one thing when one means another. It is achieved through understatement, concealment or allusion, rather than by direct statement

juxtaposition (from the Latin for 'placing next to') refers to the effects that can be gained in writing by placing unlikely events, people or places in incongruous proximity to each other

literariness a term coined by the Russian formalist critics of the 1920s to describe the ways in which literary texts habitually use grammatical structures and vocabularies that are not common to everyday speech

magic realism a kind of contemporary prose fiction in which fantastic elements are introduced into a narrative that is otherwise realistic

Marxism theories of literature, history and economics deriving from the writings of Karl Marx. Marxism emphasises the materialism of human existence, and focuses on the notion that men and women are economic animals, almost entirely at the mercy of the social and economic circumstances in which they find themselves

materialism (noun), **materialist** (adjective) the belief that life takes place only in terms of material things, that there is no spiritual dimension that might compensate, for example, for poverty or deprivation. Materialism is at the basis of Marxist and many feminist theories of literature and culture

metaphor a comparison, or fusion, in one image of two distinctive ideas or things

mock heroic the treatment of characters and events as more serious and significant than they are. The mock heroic doesn't 'mock' the idea of heroism; rather it mocks the pretensions of those who believe they are heroes when they are nothing of the kind

orality, oral narrative originally, oral narratives were spoken rather than written down. Orality now refers to the conventions in writing where the spoken word is invoked or imitated

paradox (from the Greek for 'beside opinion') an apparently self-contradictory statement or state, a statement or state of being that seems to be in conflict with logic and common sense, but which nonetheless has meaning behind its apparent absurdity

parody a mocking imitation of either a real thing or event, or of another literary work so as to ridicule the original

persona (from the Latin for 'mask') the performance of the self, as opposed to the authentic self that lies behind the mask

picaresque (from *picaro*, Spanish for 'rogue') a kind of narrative which recounts the adventures of a likeable rogue. Picaresque novels generally have an episodic structure derived from their settings on the road

polyphony (noun), **polyphonic** (adjective) (from the Greek for 'many voices') a term used by critics to describe a kind of writing in which several, sometimes contradictory, points of view coexist without being resolved to support a single authorial position

postmodernism (noun), **postmodern** (adjective) a disputed term that refers to both the content and the style of literary and other cultural artefacts. It is applied to contemporary culture to describe the ways in which that culture is fragmentary, incoherent, inauthentic, filled with parody and simulacra, and apparently has no core of shared communal values. It is sometimes used as a term of abuse, sometimes as a badge of honour

pseudonym (from the Greek for 'false name') a false or assumed identity

purple prose overblown, overwritten, exaggerated prose

realism a tendency in literature, particularly in nineteenth-century prose fiction, to portray the real world without softening its appearance. Realism aims to tell the unglossed truth about reality, though because it is a set of conventions for describing the real, it is not always particularly realistic

register a kind of language being used; in particular, the kind of language appropriate to a particular situation or context

science fiction a popular genre of modern fiction that explores the as yet unrealised potential of technological advances amongst human and non-human beings

solipsism (noun), **solipsistic** (adjective) a philosophical theory that holds that one can only truly know and prove one's own existence. All other people might exist only as a function of the solipsist's imagination

symbol an order of metaphor in which an object stands for something beyond itself, usually through well-established conventions. Where metaphor tends to operate as a comparison of one thing with one other thing, however, symbols accumulate multiple meanings

tableau vivant (from the French for 'living picture') a silent motionless person or group of people arranged to represent a dramatic scene

tabula rasa (from the Latin for 'blank tablet') a term popularised by the Romantic poets to describe the state of a newborn infant: a blank sheet of paper waiting for the world to make its impressions

uncanny the strange and the weird. The Bulgarian critic, Todorov, describes the uncanny as referring to those apparently unnatural events that actually have a psychological explanation. In addition, Sigmund Freud saw the uncanny as the effect that occurs when something non-human appears to be human, or when something human takes on the attributes of an object

utopia (from the Greek for 'no place') the term used to describe the fictional representation of worlds that are better than the one we actually live in

verisimilitude (from the Latin for 'true-seeming') the ways in which a literary text might attempt to persuade readers of its truthfulness in its depiction of the appearances of things and characters

vernacular the language of the common people. Originally used to designate any non-classical language, now used to describe the ordinary, often vulgar, language of ordinary people

Ruth Robbins is Lecturer in English at University College Northampton. She received her degrees from the University of Warwick. She is the author of *Literary Feminisms* (Macmillan, 2000), and has published a number of articles on the *fin-de-siècle* period.

York Notes Advanced (£3.99 each)

Margaret Atwood
Cat's Eye

Margaret Atwood
The Handmaid's Tale

Jane Austen
Mansfield Park

Jane Austen
Persuasion

Jane Austen
Pride and Prejudice

Alan Bennett
Talking Heads

William Blake
Songs of Innocence and of Experience

Charlotte Brontë
Jane Eyre

Emily Brontë
Wuthering Heights

Angela Carter
Nights at the Circus

Geoffrey Chaucer
The Franklin's Prologue and Tale

Geoffrey Chaucer
The Miller's Prologue and Tale

Geoffrey Chaucer
Prologue To the Canterbury Tales

Geoffrey Chaucer
The Wife of Bath's Prologue and Tale

Samuel Taylor Coleridge
Selected Poems

Joseph Conrad
Heart of Darkness

Daniel Defoe
Moll Flanders

Charles Dickens
Great Expectations

Charles Dickens
Hard Times

Emily Dickinson
Selected Poems

John Donne
Selected Poems

Carol Ann Duffy
Selected Poems

George Eliot
Middlemarch

George Eliot
The Mill on the Floss

T.S. Eliot
Selected Poems

F. Scott Fitzgerald
The Great Gatsby

E.M. Forster
A Passage to India

Brian Friel
Translations

Thomas Hardy
The Mayor of Casterbridge

Thomas Hardy
The Return of the Native

Thomas Hardy
Selected Poems

Thomas Hardy
Tess of the d'Urbervilles

Seamus Heaney
Selected Poems from Opened Ground

Nathaniel Hawthorne
The Scarlet Letter

Kazuo Ishiguro
The Remains of the Day

Ben Jonson
The Alchemist

James Joyce
Dubliners

John Keats
Selected Poems

Christopher Marlowe
Doctor Faustus

Arthur Miller
Death of a Salesman

John Milton
Paradise Lost Books I & II

Toni Morrison
Beloved

Sylvia Plath
Selected Poems

Alexander Pope
Rape of the Lock and other poems

William Shakespeare
Antony and Cleopatra

William Shakespeare
As You Like It

William Shakespeare
Hamlet

William Shakespeare
King Lear

William Shakespeare
Measure for Measure

William Shakespeare
The Merchant of Venice

William Shakespeare
A Midsummer Night's Dream

William Shakespeare
Much Ado About Nothing

William Shakespeare
Othello

William Shakespeare
Richard II

William Shakespeare
Romeo and Juliet

William Shakespeare
The Taming of the Shrew

William Shakespeare
The Tempest

William Shakespeare
Twelfth Night

William Shakespeare
The Winter's Tale

George Bernard Shaw
Saint Joan

Mary Shelley
Frankenstein

Jonathan Swift
Gulliver's Travels and A Modest Proposal

Alfred, Lord Tennyson
Selected Poems

Alice Walker
The Color Purple

Oscar Wilde
The Importance of Being Earnest

Tennessee Williams
A Streetcar Named Desire

John Webster
The Duchess of Malfi

Virginia Woolf
To the Lighthouse

W.B. Yeats
Selected Poems

Jane Austen
Emma

Jane Austen
Sense and Sensibility

Samuel Beckett
Waiting for Godot and
Endgame

Louis de Bernières
Captain Corelli's Mandolin

Charlotte Brontë
Villette

Caryl Churchill
Top Girls and *Cloud Nine*

Charles Dickens
Bleak House

T.S. Eliot
The Waste Land

Thomas Hardy
Jude the Obscure

Homer
The Iliad

Homer
The Odyssey

Aldous Huxley
Brave New World

D.H. Lawrence
Selected Poems

Christopher Marlowe
Edward II

George Orwell
Nineteen Eighty-four

Jean Rhys
Wide Sargasso Sea

William Shakespeare
Henry IV Pt I

William Shakespeare
Henry IV Part II

William Shakespeare
Macbeth

William Shakespeare
Richard III

Tom Stoppard
Arcadia and *Rosencrantz and
Guildenstern are Dead*

Virgil
The Aeneid

Jeanette Winterson
*Oranges are Not the Only
Fruit*

Tennessee Williams
Cat on a Hot Tin Roof

Metaphysical Poets

GCSE and equivalent levels (£3.50 each)

Maya Angelou
I Know Why the Caged Bird Sings

Jane Austen
Pride and Prejudice

Alan Ayckbourn
Absent Friends

Elizabeth Barrett Browning
Selected Poems

Robert Bolt
A Man for All Seasons

Harold Brighouse
Hobson's Choice

Charlotte Brontë
Jane Eyre

Emily Brontë
Wuthering Heights

Shelagh Delaney
A Taste of Honey

Charles Dickens
David Copperfield

Charles Dickens
Great Expectations

Charles Dickens
Hard Times

Charles Dickens
Oliver Twist

Roddy Doyle
Paddy Clarke Ha Ha Ha

George Eliot
Silas Marner

George Eliot
The Mill on the Floss

Anne Frank
The Diary of Anne Frank

William Golding
Lord of the Flies

Oliver Goldsmith
She Stoops To Conquer

Willis Hall
The Long and the Short and the Tall

Thomas Hardy
Far from the Madding Crowd

Thomas Hardy
The Mayor of Casterbridge

Thomas Hardy
Tess of the d'Urbervilles

Thomas Hardy
The Withered Arm and other Wessex Tales

L.P. Hartley
The Go-Between

Seamus Heaney
Selected Poems

Susan Hill
I'm the King of the Castle

Barry Hines
A Kestrel for a Knave

Louise Lawrence
Children of the Dust

Harper Lee
To Kill a Mockingbird

Laurie Lee
Cider with Rosie

Arthur Miller
The Crucible

Arthur Miller
A View from the Bridge

Robert O'Brien
Z for Zachariah

Frank O'Connor
My Oedipus Complex and Other Stories

George Orwell
Animal Farm

J.B. Priestley
An Inspector Calls

J.B. Priestley
When We Are Married

Willy Russell
Educating Rita

Willy Russell
Our Day Out

J.D. Salinger
The Catcher in the Rye

William Shakespeare
Henry IV Part 1

William Shakespeare
Henry V

William Shakespeare
Julius Caesar

William Shakespeare
Macbeth

William Shakespeare
The Merchant of Venice

William Shakespeare
A Midsummer Night's Dream

William Shakespeare
Much Ado About Nothing

William Shakespeare
Romeo and Juliet

William Shakespeare
The Tempest

William Shakespeare
Twelfth Night

George Bernard Shaw
Pygmalion

Mary Shelley
Frankenstein

R.C. Sherriff
Journey's End

Rukshana Smith
Salt on the Snow

John Steinbeck
Of Mice and Men

Robert Louis Stevenson
Dr Jekyll and Mr Hyde

Jonathan Swift
Gulliver's Travels

Robert Swindells
Daz 4 Zoe

Mildred D. Taylor
Roll of Thunder, Hear My Cry

Mark Twain
Huckleberry Finn

James Watson
Talking in Whispers

Edith Wharton
Ethan Frome

William Wordsworth
Selected Poems

A Choice of Poets

Mystery Stories of the Nineteenth Century including The Signalman

Nineteenth Century Short Stories

Poetry of the First World War

Six Women Poets